REVIEWERS' COMMENTS

'Superlative praise for Point to Counterpoint! This book has been written by a person who has lived and paid attention. Mel has skillfully pared language down to express complex insights and feelings. He offers new perspectives in poems and inspirational quotes that invite readers to reflect on their own memories, passions and experiences that may seem familiar.

The organizing principle allows readers to easily enter, engage and appreciate, any of the eleven chapters without prior reading of previous chapters. Readers, rather than reading sequentially, may prefer to enter a topic of immediate interest such as 'Parenting', 'Love', 'Sexuality and Erotic Awakenings', 'Colors and Emotions', 'Hope and Inspiration', 'Gifts of Nature', 'Existential Moments', 'Growing Old', or 'Dying and Death'.

The evocative language, kindness of tone and format of content blend artfully together, delivering a thought-provoking volume.' **Editor's Review.**

"Point to Counterpoint is a singular achievement in poetic expression; quite extraordinary in conception and execution. It is not just another book of poetry. This compilation of poems, reflections and inspirations will take readers on a journey of beginnings and endings, from birth to death and various points in between. It offers a smorgasbord of perspectives and experiences from which readers can choose. Mel has dared to create something that differentiates itself - in structure and premise - from other collections of poems I have read over decades.

Poetry is a very personal thing, both in the writing and reading. What Mel has crafted is worth spending time with. You can choose to read some or all of the poems and/or contemplate the reflections, lyrics and 'Food for Thought' presented throughout. Each of us brings our own appetite when engaging with a book, sifting through our preferences - sort of like panning for gold nuggets. Readers will find many such gems in this unique contribution to poetic literature." **Jim Sellers, connoisseur extraordinaire of art, painting, writing and poetry**

"Mel's book offers a plethora of feelings and meditations, often presented with alternative perspectives. The chapter introductions lure readers in and then let them feel and think about what has been said. The finished product emerges as the poetic art of its creator." **Dr. (Hon) Bernard Aimé Poulin, painter, poet, author, sculptor and teacher of international renown**

"This colorful compilation invites the reader on a journey; carving and painting a space for discoveries in sometimes mystical and transcendent expressions, compelling us to lean in, to marvel at, and revel in the cracks and crevices that leave an indelible mark as the years stretch and expand, and wisdom and light that is garnered through love and loss, seeps in." **Caroline Nevin, painter, fine artist, creative writer**

"I find Mel's poetry very emotionally charged, evoking many memories and even tears when I read and visualize these memories of familiar people, places and feelings. His talents have blown me away. The structure of the poems and chapters flow well. The footnotes, quotations and references are relevant and interesting.

The poems are beautiful and vivid and so very candid. I envy how he expresses himself and reveals his innermost thoughts and experiences. Many of us have similar thoughts and experiences but cannot express or communicate them." **John Yarske, Former CEO, Health Care, Sask., Alta and B.C.**

"A vicarious journey through life...Joy, sorrow and passion described with raw intensity. This intimate journey is powerfully honest and humbling." **Sylvia Nagy, Former Director of Nursing, N. B. Sask.**

"Mel's poems brim with meaning and heart. An eloquent illustration of the love story that has changed his life, charged with emotion and inspiration. **Anthea Brown, Spa/Massage Therapist who infuses her sessions with poetry recitations built on a life-long passion for poetry, song, and Greek Mythology**

Mel continues to delight and surprise - after 35 years of knowing Mel as a friend and colleague I recently learned he was also a poet with depth, tenderness and timeliness. Mel's poems speak of life, love, loss and joy and always leave you with a thought or feeling that lingers long after the reading. **Judy Bader, Former Director, Community Services and Housing, NWT, Calgary and Vancouver**

"Kudos, Mel! You've filled this book with heart and soul." **Lorraine Scory, former long-term magazine editor**

"In Point to Counterpoint Mel Gill offers his "...poetic reflections on life, love and passion" He has produced, in his own words, a book of "...compelling...deeply personal, experiences....." Would that we all might have such access to a lifetime of readings, writings, jottings and thoughts.

Mel quickly launches his theme, 'every beginning contains the seeds and signs of its own ending', preparing a vantage point for the book's unfolding. While passing through the stages and events of his own life, Mel muses on this interconnection. He frequently looks up and out to explore the universality of his theme through the minds of others. Freely declaring that he, like other thinkers, is a conduit for the gifts of wisdom from unknown sources he writes, "The poems do not belong to me". Yet his writing is clear: "This is my life as I am living it!"

Some might find the most personal of the poems uncomfortable in their frankness. Honestly revealing his own vulnerability, he exposes not only his but the intimate experiences of others. In doing so Mel has demonstrated considerable courage, exposing both his fragility and his strength." **Kent Swinburne, Former Court-appointed Family Mediator and lifelong connoisseur of poetry**

"Mel captures and blends the essences of love, life and spirit in his work, allowing the reader to reconnect with their spirit and the wonder of life, while touching the deeper and often slumbering subtleties of the heart. My own affinity for eagles was deeply touched by 'Ruler of the Skies' written in Daphne's voice. It is a deeply personal account of the authors' own connections with this majestic 'spirit bird'." **Elissa Michaud, brings a lifelong passion for poetry into her work as a spa therapist and into her life**

"An enjoyable read. I particularly like the parts where Mel has merged philosophy, spirituality and humanity into often unpredictable verse." **David Grantham, Musician, President, Friends of the Family Support Services, Victoria**

MEL D GILL

POINT
TO
COUNTERPOINT

poetic reflections
on life, love and
passion

Synergy
Associates

synergyassociates.ca

Cover photo: Dr. David Jordan

ISBN
978-1-9992303-2-6 (Hardcover)
978-1-9992303-0-2 (Paperback)
978-1-9992303-1-9 (eBook)

Key Words
birth to death; Canadian poetry; colors and emotions; beginnings to endings; reflections on life, love and passion; inspirational and mystical; sexuality and eros

BISAC code
POE 011000 Poetry, Canadian
OCC 019000 Body, Mind & Spirit, Inspiration & Personal Growth
POE 023020 Poetry, subjects & themes / Love and Erotica

Discounts may be available for volume purchases in excess of 5 copies. Please contact the author for details at mel.gill@synergyassociates.ca

DEDICATION

We've come full circle. A journey that began decades ago.
My first love and love of my life.
Not always on my mind, but always in my heart.
The inspiration for this book.
Daphne McDonald.

Together again.
Now whole!
Complete!

Thank you, Darling!

I have always loved you, *Mel*

FOREWORD

Mel Gill's book, *Point to Counterpoint*, is about a human journey from birth to death. It embraces one of the great paradoxes of art; how the artist's perspective and feelings change from the time of the art's creation to later reflection. Mel knows that he and his perceptions of his poems will change over time. He knows that the mental energy of creating art, like the physical energy of fire, is transformed but never lost. The artist creates the deliciously flammable, combustible material of which the artist and the creation are made.

Mel's poems are a joy to read. I am particularly moved by the skill of a poet who suggests the unknown, the mythical, the ethereal by using concrete images and human history in a straightforward way.

As one example of his poems, Lake Alma offers an evocative landscape in which the people, like writing itself, are born to the land and die like the speechless wind; like the sound and feel of the words that describe them, the memory of these 'spectre people' is reborn, many times as large, in the imagination of the reader.
Geoff Laundy Poet, Author, Videographer

LAKE ALMA (NEAR WEYBURN, SASKATCHEWAN 1969)

People are born here
People die
Some live scarcely more
Than a shadow existence

Mere
Spectres

Tossed about
In the speechless winds and
Drifting sands that
Sweep across
The uneasy, lonely
Beauty
Of

Lake Alma hills

CONTENTS

GREEK INFLUENCES

Concepts of democracy, rule of law, equality of citizens (males only), the foundations of Western philosophy, and Greek Mythology have had an enduring impact on civilization. You will find many words of Greek philosophers in this book. You will also find the influence of Greek Mythology, so rich in metaphors and images.

These permeate contemporary literature, art, painting, sculpture, astronomy, culture, music (muses, Apollo, Medusa, Missionary Man, Venus), movies (Spartacus, Troy, Titans, Odysseus, Immortals, Argonauts). Think of the thunderbolt of Zeus. Think of 'zodiac' constellations like Cassiopeia; the winged horse, Pegasus; Andromeda and Hercules that lead young people as aspiring astronauts, astrologists or others to gaze in awe at the stars and wonders of the universe.

Remember 'cupid', son of Mercury and Venus in Roman mythology and Eros, son of Aphrodite and Ares in Greek Mythology. Eros is the subject of Chapter Three, Love, and in Chapter Four erupts into Sexuality and Erotica.

Mythology pervades many aspects of our language, like the half-man, half-goat Pan as the source of the words 'panic' and 'panpipes'. Some of the many other words derived from names of Greek gods are atlas, chronology, narcissism, kaleidoscope, erotic, hypnosis, chaos, and typhoon.[2] Edith Hamilton

Greek mythology inspired the cover photo and one narrative thread in this book. It is particularly evident in the cupid references in poems and graphics, in the 'Sea's Garden Coral' verse of 'The Painter's Palette' and the 'Tribute to Roy'.

THE MAKING OF A POEM

Poets and writers throughout history have put their imprints on many of the topics explored in this book. The poems I offer here are my contribution to poetic literature. The quotations that follow provide a sampling of philosophers, scientists and artists who have found the making of a poem a rather mystical experience, words often seeming to flow through them.

"It was not wisdom that enabled poets to write their poetry, but a kind of instinct or inspiration, such as you find in seers and prophets who deliver all their sublime messages without knowing in the least what they mean." [3] Socrates

"My brain is only a receiver. In the Universe, there is a core from which we obtain knowledge, strength, and inspiration. I have not penetrated into the secrets of this core, but I know that it exists." [4] Nikola Tesla

"God speaks and I hold the pencil that writes what he speaks." [5] Mary Stevenson

"An artist is simply a vehicle through which an emerging vision passes." [6] Bernard Poulin

'Most often when I'm writing, I simply feel like a 'conduit' for some ethereal force.' [7] Paul Simon

Most of my poems transfer from a similar ethereal force into finished form requiring little or no editing. Others like 'The Painter's Palette' in Chapter 5 and 'Point no Point' in Chapter 6 require a good deal more work.

INTRODUCTION

"What the caterpillar calls the end, the world calls a butterfly." [8] Lao Tzu

"I am Alpha and Omega, the beginning and the ending,
saith the Lord." [9] The Holy Bible

<u>Point to Counterpoint</u> offers compelling, sometimes deeply personal, experiences as it wanders through a journey from birth to death, beginnings to endings, Alpha to Omega in poems, reflections, inspiration and Eros; experiences of life, love, passion, obsession, depression and transcendence. The book suggests sometimes countering perspectives on these. Such contrasts are even found within some of the individual poems and essays.

This book is premised on the notion that '**every beginning contains the seeds** <u>and</u> **signs of its own ending.**'

"They say the moment that you're born
Is when you start to die
And the first time that we said hello
Began our last goodbye"
[10] Roger Whittaker

Our existence on this planet is but a brief spark of life that dies almost in the same instant that it's born. I have spent a lifetime looking for answers to the meaning of existence and other deep mysteries of life.

In my pre-pubescent years, I became a curator of quotes searching for answers to these questions. In my teens and early twenties, philosophers and poets (like Aristotle, Shakespeare, Russell) stimulated my mind, touched my soul. The musings of others on a similar journey also fueled my explorations.

My earliest poems, like those of many poets, were often written on the backs of placemats, napkins, and scraps of paper. I had forgotten many of these until I gathered them for compilation into this book.

I wrote my own epitaph at age seventeen. You might ask: 'What was a seventeen-year old boy from small town Saskatchewan doing writing his own Epitaph? Certainly, it came from pondering the meaning of life. But again, the words seemed to flow through me, the poem containing its own beginning and ending, affirming the basic premise of this book.

The 'Epitaph' starts with the demise of ego, the soul drifting into the cosmos. In that sense the end (of ego) is at the beginning, while the beginning of egoless follows with release of the spirit into the universal unconscious. The poem, slightly adapted for my wife, Judith Gill, upon her death, can be found in Chapter 11.

As I was compiling the poems, I was suddenly struck by a revelation (tears now flowing), an epiphany of sorts...these poems don't even belong to me, they belong to some other source or force and I just held the pencil, as fourteen-year-old Mary Stevenson said of writing 'Footprints'.

Many years after I began this journey, I awakened one morning...and looking in the mirror, saw two visages: inspiration and poet, muses both; now indistinguishable one from the other, at times seeming to mystically merge into one.

Many of my poems have an unexpected ending, a bit like the three-line, seventeen syllable Haiku poems. Unlike the Haiku poems, mine are preceded by a sometimes-lengthy lead. They begin with pleasant, sometimes pastoral, scenes and end with a sharp, unanticipated ending. The poems that follow this pattern reflect the premise of the book, that 'every beginning contains the seeds and signs of its own ending'.

Readers may find that lines in some poems have a different nuance when read in conjunction with the previous line as opposed to the line following. The same may be found between three words within a line. Cadence may often be found reading the last few words of one line with the first words of the following line.

Many philosophers, Greek, Middle Eastern, European, American, Asian and Oriental influenced my personal philosophy and inspired my poetic journey. You'll see sprinklings of these throughout this book.

It contains brief excerpts from poems and lyrics of others. Unless otherwise noted, all the other poems flowed through my hand.

Each chapter in this book begins with a brief overview of the theme, followed by my poems and ends with 'Food for Thought' quotations or narratives intended to stimulate personal reflection, introspection or meditation.

I hope you find that the book fulfills this promise to stimulate; that you will enjoy the read and find it insightful.

Thank you for joining me on this poetic journey through 'beginnings to endings', 'birth to death', 'Alpha to Omega'.

Mel Gill

PREFACE

how fortunate you are and i, whose home
is timelessness: we who have wandered down
from fragrant mountains of eternal now
to frolic in such mysteries as birth
and death, a day (or maybe even less)
e.e. cummings [10]

CHAPTER 1
BIRTH

"New beginnings are often disguised as painful endings." [1] Lao Tzu

"The beginning and endings of all human undertakings are untidy." [2]

John Galsworthy

Conception is generally viewed as the very beginning of life, though not sustainable until about ten or twelve weeks. Scientific studies also confirm that influences outside the womb, like the mother's heartbeat, music or traumatic events can influence the child in the womb. There is anecdotal evidence of very young children seeming to have detailed recollections of past lives... often referred to as reincarnated 'old souls'.

But the poems in this chapter begin with the birth of my son, Trent, followed by a light parody of the Robert Service poem: 'Cremation' of Sam McGee.[3] Both introduce a bit of levity and show that poetry can be fun and funny with just a bit of poetic license.

These are followed by my poetic reflections on the early years of life.

I hope these shine some light on our (we humans') progression through early childhood. I've also reflected on the high standards poet and author Rudyard Kipling set for all of us in his poem 'IF'. [4] (Kipling's award of the Nobel Laureate for Literature in 1907 was indicative of the norms of the time.)

TRENT'S THANK YOU

To all the doctors and nurses who provided
Care for my mommy and me during and after my birth

If I weren't just
Too little to speak
I'd talk and tell you this
Many thanks
For my life
For my health
And thanks for
My Mommy's too
You were sharp and alert
With your knowledge and skill
Compassionate still
I can scarcely show
At my tender age
Gratitude's replete
Best Wishes
For your future
For the infants
Mothers and fathers
Whose needs you will meet

Trenton Blake Gill, Dec 23, 1974
University Hospital, Saskatoon, Saskatchewan
P.S. I had a little help from my Dad with this.

'CREATION' OF SAM MCGEE

This is the story of Sam McGee
How that legend came to be

Now Sam started out as a tiny seed
In his mother's womb – a woman's need
Along came Pappy
Warmed things up
So, Sam could sprout

Wasn't long 'fore Sam had limbs
He stretched and kicked
Asked to get out
One cold winter's night
The heat had flamed out

Sam broke into this world
Started to shout
Mom didn't like it so
She kicked Sam out

He packed his bottles
Started to crawl
To the Northern reaches

Packed on his hip were
His diaper breeches
Bottles in his pack
Soother In his mouth…
'Case he'd need to turn back

Sam traded his soother for
A fat cigar
Traded his bottles for
Whisky in a jar

Sam left a tale in the midnight sun
That would redden your ears
Before it's begun

Down went the sun
Service brought Sam
To the northern frost

Cremated Sam and
This yarn of Sam's
Early years
Nearly was lost

A LITTLE BOY

A Little Boy is
    Jelly on his face
    Dirt under his nails
    A patch on his knee
    String trailing from
    One pocket and
    A frog in the other

A little boy is
    A bag of marbles in
    His right hand and
    Licorice in the left

He's a cowboy today
    And a spaceman tomorrow
    He's mud-puddles and
    Clothespin boats

A Mother's joy
    And her sorrow
    A little boy is the angel with
    Scrubbed face and tired smile
    Who blesses mommy and daddy
    In prayers every night
    And he's the arms that
    Hug you tight

As you tuck him
    Into bed and
    Kiss goodnight

A POEM

A poem is a little girl
   Helping Mommy with the dishes
     Or teaching her how to use
       A new computer app
A little boy at play
   In his sandbox
     Or the games apps on his i-pad
A poem is
   Mommy kissing Dad
It's the sun rising in the morning
   A harvest moon at night
A poem is twinkling stars
   Over motor cars
     On bustling highways
It's city lights and airplanes
   Satellites at night
     Aurora Borealis unexpected
A poem is rhyme without reason
   And deer out of season
It's puppy dogs at play
   And swans in flight
It's all the good things in life
   And some of the bad
For a little boy, it's the moments
   Shared with Dad
A poem is a vast unending river
   Roaming quietly through the day
     And growing still in the dusk

As it gently threads its
     Present to the past
And a poem is
     You in the fullness of life

BOYHOOD DREAMS

A wellspring of
Eternal joy
Unfolds within
A little boy
He schemes and
Dreams in
Fantasies
Things no man
Could ever be
But somewhere in
His youthful eye
The boy must know
The man will die

LITTLE PEOPLE SMILE

The Little People
Smile
Their smiles beguile
Hands on hips
Head cocked
Give-way gleam in
Twinkling eyes
Spread to share
Secret mischief
Innocently radiant
Beaming face
A face of
Uncorrupted
Paradise
Little people
Smile
But not for long
Little people
Don't grow up
They die
Into an 'adult' world
Where often as not
The smiles
Are smiles defiled

THE FLOWERING OF MANKIND

The flowering of
  Mankind began
From a tiny little cell
  In self-directed
Transmutation
  Evolution
      Procreation
No longer left to
  Self-direction
The quiet little cell
    Receded into obsolescence
      Reluctant acquiescence
As the flower
  Turned to weed
      From that quiet little seed
Procreation hovered in
  Predilected indecision
      Between
Methodical salvation or
  Un-resurrected
      Self-damnation
The devil laughs in
  Foul derision

PRAIRIE MELANCHOLY

(1968 DAPHNE MCDONALD PSYCHOTHERAPIST, CREATIVE WRITER, MUSICIAN)

Unfulfilled, unspoken,
Unknown dreams
Discontent in your face
Ennui in your voice.

The hills of your home
Mesmerized stillness in me.
Absorption – within, without
Knowing you as part of that land.

Nearly a vision.
Inanimate, barren, movement-less land
While the void teemed
With human forming, striving, despair

Do you still go home
To touch the land
That formed you?
Be still …
Listen to the void!

FATHER OF THE MAN

One day soon
    In life's short span
You will become
    The man
        That you can be

Our dreams of life are
    Most times dreams
Too seldom
    Realities

Yet life sans dreams…
    A life lived sadly
    In the past
So, dream
    My son
Write your script
    It is given
        Only to you

Take pride my son in
    What you've become

The child within
    Dreams the dreams
        We are
The dreams
    Become
Father of
    The man

Through the years
You'll change and
Grow
Your seed of life
Will spread deep roots
To hold a
MIGHTY TREE

FOOD FOR THOUGHT

'IF' by Rudyard Kipling

Kipling sets a high bar for a child to become a man. Presence of mind, trust in self, patience, humility, confronting dreams with reality, taking risks, perseverance in the face of many obstacles, maintaining your values and virtue.

The last verse sets a high standard for becoming a 'man':

> *"If you can fill the unforgiving minute*
> *With sixty seconds' worth of distance run,*
> *Yours is the Earth and everything that's in it,*
> *And - - which is more - - you'll be a Man, my son!"* [4] Kipling

Kessinger, in her poem 'Indispensable Man' offers this advice:

> *"Do just the best that you can*
> *Be proud of yourself but remember*
> *There's no indispensable man."* [5] Kessinger

Fifty years ago, my first love gave me a copy of the 'Indispensable Man'. It rebuked my arrogance, sense of self-importance and made me realize how infinitely small, smaller than a speck of sand in the deserts of time, that I and other fellow travelers on this planet really are.

CHAPTER 2
PARENTING

The challenges of parenting are enormous, even more so now in times of changing roles, demographics, women pursuing careers, equality in every way with men, the 'MeToo' movement, and anxiety-producing disruption of the world order.

This chapter starts with the essence of Khalil Gibran's poem 'On Children' from The Prophet. My tributes to parents follow. The full text of Gibran's poem and excerpts from Dorothy Law Nolte's reflections on 'Children Learn What They Live' conclude this chapter.

Gibran's 'On Children' calls on parents to be procreators and sustainers, not possessors; stabilizers and guides to encourage their children's growth and individuality.

> *"Your children are not your children.*
> *They are the sons and daughters of*
> *Life's longing for itself"* [1] Kahlil Gibran

Similar words from Lao Tzu,

> *"Be parent, not possessor,*
> *Attendant, not master,*
> *Be concerned not with obedience but with benefit,*
> *And you are at the core of living."* [2]

HENRY GILL (MY FATHER)

Henry, Henry, Henry
How many different ways I've
Heard your name so spoken
 By mother, family, friends, neighbors...

Father...Dad...Daddy...Grandpa...Brother...
Friend
Words of love, respect and praise from
 Those who grew
 In the embrace
Of your kind and gentle soul
 Nurtured by love and compassion
 Guided by a quiet wisdom
 A model of Perseverance
  Courage and Respect
Always quietly
 Without aggression
 Slow to advise or criticize
Always calm in
 Temperament and demeanor
You bore your troubles
 And your pain
Silently,
 Without complaint
And in the end
 Looked Homeward
Seeking release
 Through tears you'd
 Seldom shed

MY FATHER

Father
You're gone
Yet how I long

For one last
Fleeting glimpse
Caress or smile

Some quiet reassurance
You still prevail

Yet frightened
That you might
So reappear

Not certain
I could cope
Still
    All I've left
Are memories
      And
        HOPE!
For some future

    Chance encounter of

    Our Souls

ODE TO FATHERS

Father – thy name is Strength
Courage
Wisdom

Forever art thou the castle
And the Fortress
Of my Faith

Thy name shall be eternal
Within the Mansions
Of my many Dreams

They are your Dreams
And my life
Is your life

Even unto infinity

As the seed gently planted in the soil
Lives and Dies
And lives yet more…

So do the Hopes and Aspirations
Of Fathers live in
Their Sons

And Time Honors them!

ODE TO MOTHERS

MOTHER – thy name is Blessed
For thou art the
Nurture of the Soil
Fruit of Love
Product of Thy Womb

Thou art the comfort of
The Soul

None is more blessed by
Israel than art thou

MOTHER

Thou art the Progenitor of
The Universe

The Mistress of the
Future

And time honors you!

ODE TO PARENTS

To a mother and father
   So loving and true
Sacrificing, giving
   A wonderful two

Two lives in this life
   That have meant more to me
Than words in a lifetime
   Ever could be

Your love and your laughter
   Your smiles and your tears
The sorrows and heartaches
   You've known through the years

All these and the lines
   Time never erases
I remember and cherish
   When I envision your faces

APOLOGY

I'm Sorry for
The disappointments Dad
The things I'm not
    But might have been
The doctor, lawyer
    Head of State
The things I promised
    As a neonate
You've been more
    Than patient
A friend, companion
    Confidant
No criticism
    Nor harsh reproach
Yours the kind, the gentle
    The calm approach
You've shared your life
    And sacrificed
An overflowing measure of
    Your love
If the measure of
    My fatherhood
Is someday half
    The price you've paid
I'm sure my sons
    Will then feel
About their father
    As I do You
Everlasting Gratitude and Love! Mel

'ON CHILDREN' [3] KAHLIL GIBRAN

Your children are not your children.
They are the sons and daughters of Life's longing for itself.
They come through you but not from you,
And though they are with you, yet they belong not to you.

You may give them your love but not your thoughts.
For they have their own thoughts.
You may house their bodies but not their souls,
For their souls dwell in the house of tomorrow,
which you cannot visit, not even in your dreams.
You may strive to be like them but seek not to make them
like you.
For life goes not backward nor tarries with yesterday.

You are the bows from which your children as living arrows are
sent forth.
The archer sees the mark upon the path of the infinite,
and He bends you with His might that His arrows may go swift
and far.
Let your bending in the archer's hand be for gladness;
For even as He loves the arrow that flies,
So, He loves also the bow that is stable.

CHILDREN LEARN WHAT THEY LIVE [4]

DOROTHY LAW NOLTE (1924-2005) AMERICAN WRITER/FAMILY COUNSELLOR

This poem and Nolte's books have inspired millions of parents around the world to reflect on and improve their parenting practices by understanding the impact of their behavior on their children. These are some of her reflections:

An atmosphere of fear generates apprehension and insecurity
Ridicule makes them shy
Encouragement gives them confidence
Sharing inspires generosity

FOOD FOR THOUGHT

"Good habits formed at youth make all the difference." [5] Aristotle

"The true meaning of life is to plant trees under whose shade you do not expect to sit" [6] Nelson Henderson

"Education is the kindling of a flame, not the filling of a vessel." [7] Socrates

> *"Behind every child*
> *Who believes in him or herself,*
> *Is a parent who*
> *Believed first!"*
>
> [8] Matthew L. Jacobson

> *"For a child, it is in the simplicity of*
> *play that the complexity of life*
> *is sorted like puzzle pieces joined*
> *together to make sense of the world."*
>
> [9] L.R. Knost

> *"Effective parenting 101*
>
> *A spoonful of sugar*
> *Makes the parenting*
> *More fun!*
> *Hug   Smile*
> *Play   Blow Bubbles*
> *Laugh   Enjoy*
> *Explore   Giggle*
> *Get messy   Dance"*
>
> [10] L. R. Knost

CHAPTER 3
LOVE

Love! The subject of myth, and art in all its forms throughout the centuries. It is the emotions felt and actions performed by someone concerned for the well-being of another person. Love involves affection, compassion, care, and self-sacrifice. Love is the cornerstone of deep and enduring emotional connections between people.

My own early experiences of love were nurtured in a closely-knit church community where family, friends, and relatives bonded in shared meals, social activities, choirs, picnics, card games, and sports. Love and sex were contained within monogamous relationships.

But, open talk about sex did not occur. It was, in fact, repressed. It was an uncomfortable subject for many of the early to mid-1900's generation. The focus for many was coping with the consequences of two world wars, the market crash in 1929, the 'dirty thirties drought, a dramatic rural to urban demographic shift, and the beginning of dramatic changes to the nature of work and gender roles.

I had the benefit of a liberal arts education not afforded to most of the previous generation. This encouraged me and others in my generation to think independently, gain an appreciation of books and poetry, and open our minds to the discovery of a whole new world of thought and perceived reality This was the incubator from which my values and interests emerged.

Every organic system strives for homeostasis. In humans, I've long characterized this as a striving for contentment, which includes intimacy and deep emotional connection on many levels.

"There is Friendship First in True Love. It comes from openness, trust, transparency, honesty, and loyalty. Love is not necessarily romantic, and romance is not necessarily sexual." Mel Gill

"True character can be more accurately discerned by how a person leaves a relationship than by how he/she entered it. Watch carefully! Each beginning contains the seeds <u>and</u> signs of its own destruction." Mel Gill

"How it improves people for us when we begin to love them!" [1] David Grayson

"To love somebody is not just a strong feeling - it is a decision, it is a judgment, it is a promise. It takes only a moment to tell someone you love them, but it takes a lifetime to prove it."[2] Eric Fromm

"Intimacy is about a lot more than sex. Real intimacy includes things like openness, honesty, closeness, warmth, trust, and vulnerability. We all crave a relationship that has those characteristics. We feel true love only when that type of intimate relationship exists.

[3] Marriage Counsellor.com

'Sex is only the shadow of intimacy; feelings are just the aroma of the flower we call love ... and flowers are not always in bloom. [4] Matthew Kelly

LIMERENCE

"Limerence is a state of mind which results from a romantic attraction to another person and typically includes obsessive thoughts and fantasies and

a desire to form or maintain a relationship with the object of love and have one's feelings reciprocated." [5] Dorothy Tennov

"Every heart sings a song, incomplete until another heart whispers back. Those who wish to sing always find a song. At the touch of a lover, everyone becomes a poet." [6] Plato

LOVE IS NOT LOVE

(EXCERPT FROM SHAKESPEARE'S SONNET 116)

"Let me not to the marriage of true minds
Admit impediments. Love is not love
Which alters when it alteration finds,
Or bends with the remover to remove."

[7] William Shakespeare

IN THESE ARMS

In these arms
As we hold
The future
Seems bold

Love is secure
When we are sure
No arms of another
Will ever recover

Every breath
That we take
The past
We'll forsake

A journey of love
Blessed from above
Almighty hands lead to
Long-promised lands

LOVE AT FIRST SIGHT

When first I looked
  Into your eyes
  I thought I was in love
Looking back now
  I know that
  It was right
It's the kind of love that
  Raindrops are made of
  On a cloudy autumn afternoon
  When the leaves hurry
  Down the streams with
  Unseen cargoes
It's the kind of love that shares
  The sparkling dance of moonbeams
  On the soft edge of night
The love of stars
  Whose light shines
  Sudden bright
At the meeting of
  Two strangers' eyes
Which told that
  Love was right

SOUL MATES

As I lie beside you
   In the dark of night
And gently touch your shiny, auburn locks
   Streetlights probing
      Gently chasing shadows
      Through the room
I am filled with wonder
   At the warmth and sweetness of
      Your slumber
At the depth
   Though not unblemished
      Calm serenity of your
Love for me
   And mine for you
The love,
   The girl
      Of my boyhood dreams
Our souls have touched and intertwined
   Created new lives and loves
      Unto infinity!

'The mutual filling of legitimate needs is the pinnacle of relationships.
This is what it means to be Soul Mates." [8] Matthew Kelly

MY HEART CRIES OUT

My heart cries out
  In rank despair
I cannot say
  How much I care
For you
  And you
    And you
Uncouth they say
  To proclaim such love
Except of course in
  Circumstances
    Dignified and
      Socially approved
Formal niceties forbid
  The thought be given voice
The hidden values of
  Social Structure
    Social stricture
  Sometimes
Imprison Love
    Outside the Soul

WALK NAKED

We have seen
Each other
Naked
Explored
Each other's
Contours
Bodies
Minds and
Spirits
No imperfection
Left to see
Embraced in
Lovers' passion
All senses
Eagerly engaged
Seen each other's
Essence
Found light to
Chase out
Darkness
Been humbled to
The core
Left nothing
To explore
Seen ourselves
Reflected
In each other's
Gaze
Only love left
To amaze

LOVE IS A FRIEND

Love is a Friend
Who smiles
Even when your
Words offend
Because she knows
You didn't mean them
Love is the melancholy beam
In forgotten eyes
Contented sighs
It's the breath of morning
On familiar lips
Caressing fingertips
Love is a journey
Through the stars
A walk among the planets
An unguided tour
Of the galaxies
It is the earth
The sky and the sea
Love is
The way life should be

NEVER LEAVE ME

You must never go away
Because I need you
It doesn't matter that I

Sometimes seem remote or
Don't respond to
Your touch

You owe me loyalty
For many years ago
You took my hand

Walked me down a path
Bordered by stars and
Flowered with love

If now I call and
You do not answer
The flowers will wilt
If not, I'll die and

If there is a God
She'll weep and
Surely damn you!

LONGING

Long ago I gave up longing
For something
I could not have
Longing for
Times gone by
Longing for
You in
A brief
Moment in time or
Tune
When I could
Hold you close
Proclaim
My love
Have love returned
Create the fertile space
That helps us grow
Longing for the
Love we once did share
Longing to feel your
Tender embrace
Your kiss upon my cheek
Your breath of
Love renewed
An Angel's breath in
Spring
How came we to
This place again
My dear?

Too much time between our
  First hello
    And greeting
      Now again
Longing for
  Just one more chance at
    Love
We both have
  Traveled far to this
    Last dance
A brief encounter
  That will prolong
    Our deepest love
One for the
  Other
Each to each and one
  Another

ANTICIPATION

Warm embrace at the airport
Passionate kiss when we escape
Trip to ocean-front resort, the point
To celebrate our love and
Passion for each other
We'll hold each other closely
We'll stand back to see the
Wonder of US in each other's eyes
Penetrate our souls
Help to make each other whole
We'll walk arm in arm or hand-in-hand
To find a better promised land
You'll rest your head upon my shoulder
My head will rest upon your lap
Caress each other's faces
Kiss softly bathed in sounds of ocean swells
Lay down the cares we've carried
Rejuvenate our love, our souls, ourselves
Soak in all our kindness, love and deep affection
We'll hold each other's gaze until we see
Reflection of our souls in each other's eyes
We'll gratefully receive the gifts of nature
Walk among the trees along the sea
View ocean life from a hundred feet above
Feeling connected in a way
Only we can see through each other's eyes
Uneasy that these scenes of nature's glory
May not endure beyond this last horizon
Where we have found each other once again

Blessed with a love that's deeper than
Either thought was possible
So thankful to have found this
Existential Love

DREAMS OF LOVE

Pondering the depth of our deep
Connections in oh so many ways
Our 'nothing is taboo' exchanges

It sometimes seems as though
We breathe the same air
Though a thousand miles apart

You floated to my arms
Like a faerie or angel in flight
Eyes pierced me with love and passion
YOU were all I had in sight

Sleepy cobwebs fell away as
Your exquisite visage, form
Erupted in my mind
Your soul lured me out of dreams

My body quivered at the
Memory of your voice, ecstatic touch
Love and lust merged into one
Like our souls those wonderous moments

Covers flung off in a
Raunchy night of lustful images
Now sustained by 'in the moment'
Phone calls, Emails, Facebook, texts

Instant gratification
Like wandering lust

Grinds up love to
Squeeze it out of life

Through meandering thoughts, I wondered
Does instant access
Diminish or enhance the longing?
The ache to fill a need?

My love for you
Cannot be suppressed
Restricted nor contained by
This tricky four-letter word to

Express a concept
Magnitudes greater than
The word 'love' itself

Only infinite space
Leaves room for love to grow
With the dazzling sparkle in your eyes
Moonbeams dancing with butterflies
And stars in a billion skies

RESCUED

She took me
  Into her home and
    Gave me strength
She took me
  Into her heart and
    Gave me love
She stayed by me
  In the depths of
    My despair
That I might
  Appreciate
    These
In equal measure

RESCUED TOO

I lifted her
 Out of poverty and
  Single parenthood
Exposed her to new
 Ideas
  Opportunities
   Adventures
She developed new
 Self-assurance
  Self-worth
   Independence
She embarked on
 A new career path that
Disappointed in its
 Male-dominant culture
Reminiscent of her past
 Harassment and abuse
Finally receded into a
 Recurring siege of anger
And depression so deep
 It almost destroyed her
And those of us
 In her orbit

LOVE LIFE

I'm in Love
Very much in love
It's a new love
A nascent love
A love
I don't yet
Know that well
How long ago
Since you had
Young love?
My love's name
Starts with 'L' and
Ends with 'E'
And in the middle
Haunts an
'IF'

SUCH A SPECIAL SOMEONE

More than 7 billion souls now Inhabit planet earth
Multi-billions more have passed to distant shores

Only one has brought me so much sorrow
Only one has brought me so much joy
Over oh so many years

Only you, Dear! Only you!
You stripped me naked to my core
Yet I still came back for more

Your love has brought me laughter
Your love has brought me tears

Your love has ripped my heartstrings
Over more than 50 years

Now we're near the ending...the last few years we have
It seems like new beginnings for a
Love that once arced brightly

Like lightning in a storm
Now chasing out the darkness
Healing wounds once deeply torn

The promise of what together we might have been
We must set aside, to let us start again
Inspired by two hearts, two souls now
deeply intertwined

I love you more than billions of other people
You amaze me! So special to me, Darling!

I am filled with gratitude to
Start this New/Old journey
Bathed in wonder and in awe

Truth be told we chose each other
No longer any other

MOST IMPORTANT PERSON

Everyone Needs
To be
Someone's
Object of attraction
Passion and obsession
Admired and adored
Beguiled
Cared for
Valued
To their core
Cherished and desired
Embraced, encouraged and excited
Hugged, held and honored
Loved above all others
Protected yet independent
Respected
Supported not neglected
Touched and treasured with
Tenderness, gratitude and grace
Walked beside
Filled with pride
As the MOST IMPORTANT
PERSON in
Their
Life

SUMMER OF OUR LOVE

The Summer of
   Our Love has gone
Winds have blown
   The sun has shone
Melancholy clouds
   Have drifted
     Sand
Has shifted
   Washboard ripples on
     Vacant shores
The seasons
   Have grown weary
     On fleeting wings of
     Haste
Leaving an empty
   Bitter taste
All that remains
   That lingers
Is the elusive
   Wistfulness of
A smile-forgotten face
For with the summer gone
   Has gone
Our love

LOVE RECLAIMED

When last we spoke
    An image came

This latest journey
    The latest challenge

That will test
    The strength of

Our RESOLVE to
    Build upon the love

Begun so long ago
    Now re-ignited

Hesitant at first like those
    First faltering steps of foals in spring

Struggling to stand
    Kicking up heels

Now thundering hoofbeats
    Racing toward an

Ever closer
    finish line

Two hearts now
    Pierced

By arrows from
A Cupid's bow

Souls now merged by
Love in overflow

Francois Gerard, 1798 Psyche (Soul/Breath of Life) receiving her first kiss from Cupid (Desire/Amor)
a symbolic butterfly (psyche in ancient Greek) hovers over Psyche in a moment of innocence poised
before sexual awakening. Louvre Museum, Salon of 1798, Oil on Canvas.
Psyche is the personification of the soul. Here, she is aroused by the touch of Cupid, whom she can
feel but not see. Gérard expresses the purity of the feeling with smooth flesh tones and modest poses,
emulating the marble sculpture by Antonio Canova (Louvre). http://cartelen.louvre.fr/cartelen/
visite?srv=car_not_frame&idNotice=16942&langue=en

LEAVE ME ALONE

Sometimes
I wish
You'd just go away
Leave me alone

And not come back…
Until I need again

Your smile
The soft caress
Of your eyes

Your silly romanticism and
Bubbling ballerina moods

That hide your unsure steps
Till tomorrow
Or maybe now

The quiet weight of your
Head on my shoulder
Night or morning

And feel
Your need
To fill mine

LOVERS' EYES

From Lofty Perch
In Lovers' Eyes
Impassioned Pearls
Of Paradise
Descend and Drift
To lower skies
From Misty Mountains
Lovers come
To Touch
To Magnify
To Bring
The Sun of
Nature's Dawn
Sweet Innocence
Anew
With Life and Love
Refreshed
For Youth
Portending
Immortality's Demise

HOW DO I LOVE YOU?

How do I love you?
  With all my heart and soul
Sometimes unsaid, unsaying, unsayable
  In all your Insecurity
    Innocence
      Naivety
In all the Uncertain Wisdom of
  My lesser years and
Uncertain soul's sojourn
I love you for
  The depth behind your eyes
    The certain confidence of
Your Temptress Face
  The warmth and desperation of
Your embrace
The surreal shimmer of your hair
  Around the
    Magnetism of your soul

Does God speak to me
  Through your Love?
Or the Devil
  Through your lies?

LOVE ME FOR WHO I AM

Donna
Large brown eyes
Wistful
Sighs
Virgin thighs
Breathtaking beauty
Pursued in lust
Wondering if it's
Really you they want
Sometimes
Sad countenance
In prayer
To be loved
Just for who you are
Rather than
How you look

HARSH WORDS OF LOVERS

Even the walls cringe at
*   Harsh words of lovers*
Children weep with anxiety
*   Because they want so much*
To understand … but can't …
*   Their love's too big!*
The bed that once shared joys
*   Stands lonely and aloof*
The walls seem not so bright
*   As yesterday when they*
*   Didn't harbor gloom*
The Godhead hangs in sorrow for
*   They'll be the same tomorrow*
The walls can bring no comfort
*   Their burden is*
Secrets they can never tell

MEET MY WIFE

Hello …. This is Judy
or Judith as she sometimes prefers
Depending on her Mood or Cycle of Emotions
And she has many

Sometimes more victim than survivor
Sadness, insecurity, ambivalence
Cloaked by an air of mystery, enigmatic beauty

Mostly calm, but occasionally
A volcanic eruption spewing spears of
Spite and uncontrolled vitriol

Too quick to proffer unsolicited advice
Lost her many friends
We share a home
A bed
A name
Some kids

Some good times, some bad
Contentment when the good shines brightly
Enough to chase away the darkest shadows

We share as much joy as we can capture
Some sorrow
As much life
As we can
Before tomorrow

Some just call her Judy or Judith
I have called her these and other
Terms of endearment… or less
But I have also called her
WIFE

LONELY TRAVELER

I am a lonely traveler
On this road to
Heartbreak and
Desire
How can I
Assure you the
Love that I require
Deep-seated need
No other creed
Grant me this 'fore
Love expires
Please grant me
My desires…
One love
One life
Together
With love and lust
Combined
In love that
Lasts forever

WHEREFORE LOVE?

"The times, they are a-changin"
Sang Bob Dylan in 1963 [8]
Woodstock 1969
Sex, drugs, rock'n roll
Casual, carnal, anonymous sex
The pill, abortion and divorce
Women freed to please
Once suppressed
Innate sexual desires
Released from shame?
Well, not quite yet!
Finding power in the
Sisterhood of 'Me Too'
Grasping for equality in
Boardroom, Bedroom, Cutting Room
In a still male-dominated culture
Easy access porn
Open marriages
Fad of 1960's and on
Who knew the consequences?
Sex in this milieu?
Let's set some rules
Protect your partner
Safe sex or
Just illusion?
HIV Aids intrudes on
Decades of unsafe sex
What could be the worry?
STDs? Who really cares?
Infect another

Just one more risk to
Reckless, careless indiscretion
Dating sites for cheaters?
Double adultery once in law [9]
Swipe for sex on Tinder
'More than a dating site
It's a cultural revolution'
Tinder claims
Objectify and denigrate
Self and other
What of respect and dignity?
Free love? Is anything really free?
Is there really a 'no consequences'
'Free lunch'?
Swingers' pretend
There is. Not so!
Wherever will this end?
Polyamorous relationships?
In every triad
One always feels left out
No rules protect against
Envy and Jealously
Dismissed? Restrained? Suppressed?
Basic human emotions Denied?
When does higher pleasure,
Cross a line to extreme
Soul destroying
Destructive obsession
Inflicting self- and other harm?
Where is love?
How can we make this right?
Is this the way to bridge

The sexual satisfaction gap
Between the genders?
Can we rescue
Our lives from ennui, from anomie?
Honor and obligation?
What of love and merging souls?
Cannot lust
Procreation
Relational bonding
Recreation be sustained
In a union of love
Between just two?

TIMELESS LOVE

I could never have expected a brief hello
So many years ago
Would bear the fruits of Eden
Yet stay so long uneaten

Quintessential love, deep
Exquisite understanding
Souls merging in and out as
Hand in hand we travel
Love, independent, yet as one

There will be more for us to explore
Immersed in the deepest
Connection that shines a quiet light...
Until the next eruption of a

Blinding stab of bright to
Illuminate the heavens, like a
Celestial shower
Waiting to alight
Upon our incandescent love.

Good night my love, my lover
I don't just love you
I'm head over heels, 'hooked' on you
Like a fish dangling on a line

I speak truth to power...and you have the
Power. It flowed from your heart to mine

Upon a Cupid's arrow
To pierce me through my heart!

LIGHT OF MY LIFE!

The candle of my love
Does not flicker
In the wind

It burns still brightly
Like the love that
Lights your eyes
Precious loving sighs

Soon we'll go to sleep
My love will be
A pillow
For your head

My arms will comfort
Tears you've seldom shed
Too painful to remember
Faint memories now instead

Since meeting
Last September
In the Autumn of
Our love

I'll touch my lips
So gently to
The light
Above your brow

We'll sing the
Songs of love
We sang these
Once before

How could we
Have forgotten
Remembering
Only now

Love we had
Before
Will last
Forevermore

I love you, Darling!

WHEN WE MAKE LOVE

When we make love
I become
An extension of
You
I lose
My identity
And drift

Like a lost traveler
Through the mystery of
Your womb

In search of myself
And eternity

MY PRAYER FOR LOVE

EMPTINESS
SORROW
HOPE
FOR A LOVE THAT
NEVER WILL BE BROKEN
MISSING YOU
MY PRAYER
FOR YOUR
RETURN

FOOD FOR THOUGHT

An attraction between people is often nearly instantaneous, in the 'blink of an eye'. It occurs in the limbic system of the brain, unrestrained by the more thoughtful neocortex. This attraction is complex; transmitted through eye contact, facial expression, body language, conformation, or symmetry, of form, lips, hair and other unconscious physical signals, including the powerful olfactory effect of pheromones. Research is only beginning to explore these subtle cues.

Commonly known as 'chemistry', it is an intensity of feelings; 'falling in love'; the passionate dance of love; procreational, relational* and recreational. But the flames of passion may diminish over time, leading some partners to engage in extramarital relationships. For others, fidelity was simply never in their nature. *(strengthening physical and emotional bonds between lovers)

'There is a restlessness within many of us that wants to be calmed, tamed. This restlessness is our heart's yearning for intimacy. In our efforts to feel complete, worthy, fulfilled and contented, we often seek pleasure, possessions, and achievements. We convince ourselves that if we experience the right type of these, the restlessness will be overcome, and we will finally have a sense of fulfillment and contentment. While each encounter can be very satisfying and emotionally releasing in that brief experience, the aftermath leaves us still yearning for something more. So, we chase more intense such experiences, yet are left with the same dissatisfied aftertaste.' [10] Matthew Kelly

A survey of research reported in Encylopedia.com indicates that an overwhelming majority of people in committed marital or dyadic relationships experience greater sexual and life satisfaction compared to other cohorts and that there is a clear link between the two.

"According to Greek mythology, humans were originally created with four arms, four legs and a head with two faces. Fearing their power, Zeus split them into two separate parts, condemning them to spend their lives in search of their other halves." [11] Plato

The following excerpts from the lyrics of songs on the topic of love are dear to my heart: 'Two hearts that beat as one'; The intense passion of "Leave me Breathless" Lost love reclaimed "You'll come to me, out of the long ago." This is our song, our experience, our love … so wonderful!

"You're every breath that I take
You're every step that I make
'Two hearts that beat as one"
[12] Lionel Richie

"Go on, come on, Leave me Breathless
The daylight's fading slowly
I'm waiting for you only
Tease me tempt me" [13] The Coors

"Somewhere, my love there will be songs to sing
Although the snow covers the hope of spring
Someday we'll meet again my love
You'll come to me out of the long ago
Warm as the wind, soft as the kiss of snow
God speed my love till you are mine again"
[14] Maurice Jarre

CHAPTER 4
SEXUALITY AND
EROTIC AWAKENINGS

"Eros drives us to transcend ourselves through desire" Oxford English Dictionary

This chapter introduces readers to more poems, drawn from my own experience and fantasies of Eros and eroticism. The lust described in these poems favors its expression within the context of loving relationships. I encourage reading this in conjunction with the 'Food for Thought' ending in the previous chapter.

"Even sex, perhaps the most primal human pleasure of all, can be appreciated in higher and lower ways. To adapt Brillat-Savarin, animals copulate, humans make love. In the intensity of sexual arousal and orgasm, it might not seem that our evolved human capacities are doing much work. But sex is highly contextual, and changes its nature depending on whether it is part and parcel of a genuine relationship between two human beings, however brief, or merely the satisfaction of a brute urge." [1] Julian Baggini,

Inspiration from song lyrics, particularly those of Rod McKuen, Leonard Cohen, and Maurice Jarre will be found in influences or excerpts from their works infused in my poetry. [2]

This chapter begins with Lee Hazlewood's 'Summer Wine'.

The chapter ends with an essay in 'Food for Thought' that discusses sexual awakening; parental influences on children that follow them into adulthood; addictions; monogamy; infidelity; open marriage and other alternate sexual lifestyles; historical abuse and subjugation of women; and, explores relative 'extremes' of human sexual behavior. It discusses the effect and causes of these behaviors and their correlation with early life and cultural influences.

SUMMER WINE

"Strawberries, cherries and an angel's kiss in spring
My summer wine is really made from all these things
Take off your silver spurs and help me pass the time
And I will give to you summer wine." [3] Lee Hazelwood

AWAKENING

Up each morning
  Before I'm out of bed
That stolid, solid
  Part of me
Raises its
  Pesky vermillion head
That makes
  My mind
Go crazy with
  Imaginings
Cravings for
  The Widow
Fertile's
  Sterile child *

*P.D. James, Children of Men, 1992 dystopian future

SIREN CALL

I thought I heard
    A distant Siren Call

Unrestrained by ties that bind
    To any passing ship or shore
        I came to see

What mischief there might be
    Moans and groans
        And thrashing limbs to

Discover a delightful creature
    At once a kid and dazzling woman

I am Victoria's best-kept Secret
    She proclaimed

Seduced and charmed
    Smitten and ensnared

I stayed a while
    To see what together
    We might be

Enchanted by beguiling smile
    Her Cheshire grin and
        Feigned innocence

Test me she challenged
    You'll see that I am real

We played and frolicked
In the rain

Harbored in between
We gazed with love
Into each other's eyes
Touched each other's souls

Held hands, held hearts
Held bodies close, nuzzled necks
Till we could no longer tell
Where each of us did end
And the other did begin

Warm caresses
Gentle Angel's Kisses
Then tongues entwined
Paused for breath
Then back again

Passion unbridled
Wide open to each other
We filled each other up

If you like it do not question
Just enjoy
She said in mild rebuke with
Same coquettish grin

We shared sorrows
Shared dreams

Shared joys
Shared overflowing love

Music playing
Hips swaying
We danced not to the end
But to the beginning of
An old love now reframed

Transformed forever
From 'each' to 'us' or 'me' to 'we'
Basking in the wonder of
What had taken place

We parted for a time
With Promise of return
Not certain
What next steps
That we might take

Took with us
A sense of each other's essence
Scent upon our lips
Down to our fingertips

To carry with us
Until we touch
We hold
Each other
Once again

MEASURE OF LOVE

Longing gaze
  Thoughts of love amaze
Tingling at tender touch
  Almost too, too much
Anticipation
  Excitation
Sensations remembered
  Minds surrendered
Arms extended
  In stark submission
Nearly breathless
  Resuscitation
Tip to toe
  Capitulation
Parts engorge
  Above below
Simply nowhere else
  To go
Heartbeats race
  To another time and place
Features flush
  Hormones gush
Bodies excited
  Now united
Souls entwined
  Love rejoined
Butterflies
  Ecstatic sighs
Passion sears
  Sudden tears

Patience, kindness
  Selflessness
Unconditional
  So traditional
Love unending
  So heart-rending
For us internal
  For time eternal

LADIES' DANCE

Like birds of paradise
  Ladies primp and
      Preen and
      Put on airs
Gliding
  Dainty entrances
Inviting
  Furtive glances and
      Open stares of
          Sex-starved men
Whose eyes
  Lust up
      With gleam
Who dream of
  Thighful bliss
      On satin sheets
The scene is set for
  Cocktail talk and
      Smoke-soft music in
          Spanish eyes
The ghost of Judy Richter
      Dies
Still the vagabond
  Within me cries
Do I dare to
  Lead the step
      Dance the dance
          Of life and love?

What manner man
Cries old John Drone
Who wants to live
His life alone?

IF YOU WILL HAVE ME

If you will have me
I will share with you
The Planets

There has never been a time
When smoke-blue eyes could not
Mystify me wholly

When you're near
My body warms at just
The promise of a touch

Wistfully I feel the
Quiet exhilaration of
Your caress upon my cheek

Your lips engulf me as
We glide secretly to another plane

My entire being
Floats upon a reservoir of sperm
Like an ineffective anesthetic
In dizzy turmoil at the center of
Your womb

And you think
I care

Your husband knows?

CATCH THE CLOUDS

Catch the Clouds
*   As they drift by*
The moist mist kissed
*   In dream-blue high*
Catch the clouds in
*   The sweet salt snare of*
A woman's womb
*   A cozy room*
Catch the clouds
*   If you dare*
Catch the moist seed
*   Plant it deep*
Bring the moist need
*   From its*
Dreamy sleep

EMBERS OF DESIRE

Fifty years ago
  Or more
Our paths
  Did intersect
In that brief moment
  Before moon's shadow
Eclipsed the sun's
  Bright rays and
Cooled the embers of
  Our love
Now reconnected
  After oh so many years
Embers reignited
  To bring the spark of love to last
We'll walk these
  Last few days we have
Together
  On a road that
Arm-in-arm we will discover
  Bathed in existential bright
That only you and
  I will see
Wounds that once were open
  Now healing... at last, at last
Darkness chased out
  By light-fueled flight
We dance between
  The moon and sun
Sway gently
  From our hips in

Beams of pure delight
I'll come to you in time
Clutch you to my body
To my soul
I'll carry you cross the
Threshold of
Ecstasy and desire that
Only lovers know

EROTICA

Early to bed
   Too soon awake
With fantasies of
   A sensuous kind
Pesky peccadillos or
   Graver sins
Like some deluded
   Don Juan de Marco
Don Quixote
   De Cervantes
Wanton, outrageous
   Russian Rasputin
Engorged on privilege
   Religious charlatanry
Seduction, sex, and alcohol
   Not yet put to rest
Thoughts turn to
   This wanton woman
Restless in my bed
   Making crazy in my head
I reach for her to find
   Scintillating sexual energy
Enough to trigger a
   Tsunami in this place, meant for
Peaceful sleep
   But not quite yet!!!

EROS

I will come to you
  In time
Excite you with
  My rhyme
We'll 'come' together...
  Ecstasy sublime
Share intimate
  Contented sighs
I'll seek
  Eros in your eyes
Worship at the altar of
  Your love
Pay homage to
  your lust
Savor
  Summer wine
At the junction of
  Your thighs
This intersection of
  Desire
Excites
  Ignites
Sets bodies
  Minds afire

ECSTASY

Bodies close, arms embrace
The dance of love begins
> *MINE: He whispers softly in her ear*
> *YOURS: She gently breathes against his lips*
Take me, take all of me they gasp
> *The steepest climb*
> *To the deepest place*
They could find
> *To realize release*
> *In body-shaking shudders*
Desire not yet sated
> *They pause a while*
> *Limbs still entwined*
Caresses warm and gentle
> *Relaxed, refreshed*
> *The dance begins again*
Excitement reignited
> *Again, again, again*
> *Until joyful, sublime they part*
Promise to return
> *A rendezvous of hearts*
> *Dance the dance again*
Another place, another time
> *Bodies to rejoin*
> *Spirits made to soar*
Pleasure to excite
> *Once more and yet*
> > *Once more!*

ALPHA TO OMG OH! MEGA

Early morning waking
> *Thoughts now overtaking*
My body and my mind
> *Thoughts of you remind*
Even in its retracted state of grace
> *This flaccid member seeks another space*
Memories of a lustful lover
> *Portend what we'll discover*
Tis not the lover's sacred face
> *It's single eye now focused on another sacred place*
Aroused it stiffens as it grows
> *Seeking G's, A's, C's and O's and Ohs!*
The mons below her belly
> *That turns a man to jelly*
Seeking penetration, penile, tongue and fingers
> *Exciting passion in sweet spots where he lingers*
Ecstasy exploding in body-quaking quivers
> *Head to toe, overarching love brings shivers*
From Alpha to Omega to OMG I'm shaking
> *This loving's been so, Oh! breathtaking*

Excerpts from lyrics and poetry on concepts of love. The first is one of the most powerful expressions of sexual energy and surrender to love and lovemaking.

POWER OF LOVE [4] JENIFER RUSH

"The whispers in the morning of lovers sleeping tight
Are rolling by like thunder now as I look in your eyes
'We're heading for something
Somewhere I've never been, sometimes I am frightened
But I'm ready to learn 'bout the power of love"

OBSESSIVE LOVE [5] EILEEN MANASSIAN GHALI

This poem contrasts lukewarm love and burning passion with images like these from a poet whose works like this, and 'Never Shame a Woman', are an uninhibited assertion of women's rights to enjoy the passions of love and lust, no less than men.

"Press not to flaming lips your tepid kiss'
'A lukewarm love can never bring to bliss
'Nor will I 'faint with weak caress'
'Seared by passion's burning might"

FOOD FOR THOUGHT

Where do babies come from, Mommy? "The stork brings them!" End of story! The more precocious child might ask: "Where does the stork get them?" A parent more comfortable with such subjects might respond: "Well, they grow from tiny seeds, like in a pea pod." That's usually more than enough to satisfy the curiosity of young children.

Humans are innately sexual beings. Awakening of sexual self-awareness in children usually begins in 'middle childhood' (children in their early school years) when they feel stimulated by touching themselves 'down there'. Generations of parents would shame their children when they discovered such activity. The default admonishment was "Stop that, it's dirty!". And that was the end of it…the beginning of repressed, then hidden, sexuality for boys and girls. A more enlightened parent might say: "That's private, keep it in a private place."

Many in my generation will remember learning the anatomy of sex from a somewhat older or better-informed friend's explications and drawings. Many will also remember 'playing doctor', an early version of show and 'don't' tell.

Pre-pubescence through early adolescence is usually accompanied by increased sexual behavior. There is often stimulation from easily accessible books like Harlequin Romances. Others such as Grace Metalious's 1956 Peyton Place exposed the sexual and moral hypocrisy of a fictional small town. The 1955 Lady Chatterley's Lover by D.H Lawrence, banned in many countries, also wound its way underground into the busy fingers of baby boomers.

The accessibility of magazines pandering sex (sometimes secretly hidden in a father's drawer) were among multiple other sources of stimulation. Masturbation was hidden 'under the sheets' or in other private places. During adolescence, the dating game provided opportunities to turn fantasies into reality. Early adulthood brought the challenges of adult social norms, responsibilities, and expectations as they evolved over time in different cultures. Behavior that was once tolerated, if not condoned, was no longer.

There are some cultures, social structures and religions that regard multiple wives and concubines as the norm. They repress and subjugate women, often inflicting violence. The punishments for transgression of these norms has always been, and continues to be, much harsher for females than males. They include public shaming, lashing and stoning. Female Genital Mutilation (FGM) is but one example still practiced today. There are nine countries that still carry a death penalty for female 'adultery'. A quick internet search will reveal the horrors of female subjugation and repression through the centuries.

Polygyny and polygamy were widely accepted in Old Testament times. "Adultery was defined as a crime against a man, either husband or father, as it still is in much of the world today, especially in regions influenced by Islam." [6] Barash and Lipton

A double standard has existed for millennia. It's the male prerogative to 'sow his oats' before making a long-term commitment. A female doing the same thing is likely to be labelled promiscuous ... good for a fling, but not the real thing. Multiple sexual partners are the 'prerogative of the penis'.

Monogamy is rare in all but a handful of lower organisms according to scientific studies reported by reputable researchers, including Barash and Lipton; "neither is monogamy ubiquitous in humans." [7] Barash and Lipton

Notwithstanding this, Barash and Lipton conclude that "No other marital pattern---polygyny, polyandry, group marriage---has been shown to work better. Nonetheless, monogamy does not work perfectly---On balance, perhaps monogamy is like Winston Churchill's description of democracy, the worst possible system," except for all the rest. [8] Barash and Lipton.

Where monogamy occurs in 'Western societies', it is often because religious or social structures favor a stable family unit to raise children. As the fertility period ends, and, in the absence of continuing attraction, sexual and life satisfaction, the ties that bind may begin to fray leading some partners to engage in extramarital relationships. For others, fidelity was simply never in their nature.

Research suggests that "Female adultery is certainly more common than we'd like to acknowledge. A 2016 Globe and Mail survey of 11,259 people found that 33 per cent of women said they'd had an affair, placing them not far behind the 40 per cent of men who admitted the same." [9] Zosia Bielski

The Kinsey Reports on research based on interviews resulted in <u>Sexuality in the Human Male</u>, (1948) and <u>Sexuality in the Human Female</u>, (1953). They challenged conventional beliefs about sexuality. Masters and Johnson used laboratory observation of actual sexual encounters to shed new light on human sexual response. Despite severe criticism [10] of their methodologies, and manipulation of data, these reports received widespread attention, and readership and had a huge influence on views of human sexuality. [10] Wikipedia; Jeffrey Escoffier.

Perhaps the most influential book on a woman's right to gender equality in sexual expression was Helen Gurly Brown's 1962 book, <u>Sex and the Single Girl</u>, early in the second half of the last century. That was followed in short order by Betty Friedan's <u>The Feminine Mystique</u> (1963).

Robert Chartham's 1971, <u>The Sensuous Couple</u>,[11] was another early entry to a series of books that explored, educated, and promoted the pursuit of sexual satisfaction in couples and experimentation with new positions and practices such as oral sex. It's reflective of the times that Penthouse International Ltd., a magazine that exploits women and aggressively promotes freedom of sexual expression, holds the copyright for this book. This was followed in 1972 by Alex Comfort's 'sex manual', <u>The Joy of Sex: A Gourmet Guide to Lovemaking</u>.[12] It promoted similar sexual practices to those in <u>The Sensuous Couple</u>. It also discussed alternative lifestyle experimentation like swinging.

'Open marriage', an alternative to monogamy, was further explored by George and Nina O'Neil in their 1972 book <u>Open Marriage: A New Lifestyle for Couples</u>. It presented guidelines intended to protect primary partners by defining boundaries around open marriage, polyandry, polygyny, polyamory, and other non-monogamous sexual lifestyles that began to emerge or reemerge in the early seventies. This book and the concept changed the perception of marriage for an entire generation.[13] George and Nina O'Neal

Rules suggested for open marriages and other multiple partner relationships include: the uncoerced, unmanipulated agreement of <u>both</u> partners to initially engage in, or continue, open relationships; honesty and transparency; safe sex; 'not in my bed'; regular testing for STIs; no emotional entanglement with another; limits on the number of encounters with any specific partner; approval of external partners; and delineating the type of sex acts which can or cannot be engaged in outside the primary relationship.

These rules, even if explicit were, as often as not, honored in the breach. They could not suppress emotions such as jealousy, envy, resentment, one partner feeling left out or betrayed. Jealousy is one of the most complex emotions; "a sickening combination of possessiveness, suspicion, rage, and humiliation that can overtake your mind and threaten your very core. The consequences can be eviscerating. It is the annihilation of self.[14] Esther Perel

Incidence rates for open marriage in the United States are not well researched, but estimates have ranged from 1.7% to 9%. The research suggests that the proportion of individuals in open marriages and other alternative sexual lifestyles is small (likely closer to 4%). The estimated failure rate is high (49 to 92%).

My wife and I considered the possibilities and the risks of open marriage in the early 1970's. We observed, in our circle of acquaintances, that those who experimented with an open marriage lifestyle failed. One partner, more often the female, was left emotionally scarred. Raising children in such an environment? Not worth the risks!

There are many factors that influence sexual behavior. No one has yet defined 'normal' sexual engagement. Norms are defined by the cultural context and that context seems to be changing. Humans will continue to experiment with alternate forms of sexual expression.

But sexual behavior, regardless of cultural context, needs special scrutiny when it objectifies or diminishes 'the other person'; leads to self-harm or harm to others; becomes obsessive in a way that disrupts usual daily activity; it stems from trauma, as is often the case; or it is fueled by other addictions. This type of behavior, at the extremes, is referred to as hypersexuality.

We are beginning to better understand the dynamics of all these competing and sometimes complementary factors influencing human sexual behavior. Brain scans show there are similar triggers for hypersexual behavior and alcoholism. While there clearly are genetic precursors for alcoholism, evidence also shows that both these and other addictive behaviors are often rooted in early childhood trauma and abuse. Adults with such a history often engage in repetitive addictive behaviors... to self-medicate stress.[15]
Lizette Borelli

To paraphrase Dr. Robert Wiess and Dr. Fran Walfish, repeated moves may create attachment disorders. And a child cannot count on stability from a parent whose emotional pendulum swings from warm and positive to harshly punitive, whether it's by hand, gesture, voice or mood. This is a major contributor to relationship difficulties in adulthood. Such parenting practices risk creating insecurity, separation anxiety, loss of self-esteem and a shame-based sense of self when children feel unloved and unlovable. [16] Wiess and Walfish

Yet some individuals are more resilient than others and manage or appear to manage the worst ravages of such abuse. A major 'resilience booster' for a child is having 'even just one' supportive adult who believes in them.

"Sex and drugs are quick dopamine enhancers. As a result, the more that addicts "yell" at their dopamine receptors, the "deafer" they become, meaning the greater their tolerance for the addiction in question.

'A sex addict said: "You try so hard to dull the pain and the shame that after a while, the only thing strong enough to get through the haze is the pain you're trying to anesthetize in the first place." [17] Ethlie Ann Vare

"Past reason hunted and, no sooner found, Past reason hated." [18] Shakespeare

Casual sex will not disappear. High tech connections are making it easier. The 'pill', along with easier access to abortion and divorce have given women more freedom to express their sexuality. However, there are still antediluvian conservative forces resisting the advance of women's equality.

'Is the golden age of online dating over?' asks <u>Gayle MacDonald, Globe, and Mail,</u> February 9, 2019

Gayle reports, from both anecdotal and scientific surveys, that many people, regardless of gender or sexual orientation, are growing increasingly distressed and dissatisfied with dating sites that match people based on various criteria, often of suspect value in matching compatible couples.

She cites a number of reputable studies, like Pew Research, that "Sixty-one percent of millennials who have never married say they would like to someday – a number that hasn't changed since the 1970s. Similarly, eight in ten millennials say that true romance is "very important".

The 'swipe for sex' culture of some dating sites, like Tinder, Grindr, Snapchat, and Instagram seems to be 'turning off' women in increasing numbers while some men are still chalking up their scores and bragging about it. Women in particular "want stability and a relationship built on trust and loyalty; substance instead of swipes."

"The swiping culture lures us with infinite possibilities, but it also exerts a subtle tyranny. The constant awareness of ready alternatives invites unfavorable comparisons and weakens commitment. "Sex, marriage, and parenthood used to be a package deal. No longer. The boomers separated sex from [love] marriage and reproduction." [19] Esther Perel

Some accept that IRL* connections are difficult to find in the busy lives of professionals. So, they see 'fast connection' dating sites as a necessary evil. Others are looking for sites or settings that offer a more organic, if not traditional, approach to assessing compatibility and forming relationships.

Futurologist, John Naisbitt, forewarned of this conundrum in his 1982 book, <u>Megatrends,</u> [20] which cautioned about the dissonance between 'High Tech, Low Touch' and the future impact of technology on human relationships.

* IRL – 'In Real Life' As distinguished from actual events, people, and activities from fictional worlds or characters, from interactions on the Internet, or, pejoratively, from certain lifestyles or activities that the speaker deems less important, worthy, or otherwise "real.".

CHAPTER 5
COLORS AND EMOTIONS

The intense relationship between colors and emotions is reflected in art, sculpture, painting, literature, music, movies, psychology, chakras, branding, marketing and more. I've tried to capture some of this in 'The Painter's Palette" along with the other poems in this chapter.

"Like others before me, I have the gift of sight, but the truth changes color, depending on the light, and tomorrow will be better than yesterday." [1] Eve's Bayou, movie

"All our knowledge has its origins in our perceptions." [2] Leonardo Da Vinci

KALEIDOSCOPE OF EMOTIONS

Kaleidoscope of emotions
Like a leaf
Tossed about in the
Unrelenting tide of
Human evolution
Fickle
    Incomprehensible
       Heart-rending
         Heart-mending
Once here
    Once there
Then neither here
    Nor there
One moment on the
    Tip of tongue
Choked by
    Joy or
       Sadness
Then dancing elusively
    Vanishing
Tangled in superlatives too
    Elevating or
       Deflating
Constant struggle for
    Equilibrium
Beyond imagination
    Swimming through
Despair to
    Euphoria
Back again

Again, and again
Looking for our core
Has Death the only key
   That unwinds this
Corkscrew
   Maze of emotions?

SOUL-DESTROYING HATE

To sleep or to wake on
  A mattress of hate
Rest you need or
    The trusty steed of
      Your mind
Will falter
    Break its halter
      Ties that bind
Definitive statements
    I cannot make
My mind
    Will break
In sleep I'll
    Seek the dim
      Oasis of Oblivion
On the dark and
    Soul destroying
      Forlorn sheets of
      Hate
      OR
    Purification
      On reborn sheets of
Everlasting LOVE

SPECTRE OF DEPRESSION

Thanatos or Eros
    Instinctive choice
The Spectre of Depression
    Stealthily awaits
One second of self-pity
    To grasp its victim's mind
Drag and flog him to
    Submission at
Death's too eager
    Too soon open gate
He musters up resistance
    With that other instinct Life
New resolutions – struggle for
    Appreciation, wonder, being
Silent ends
    New beginnings
Unforeseen
    The future
Still hidden
    From our eyes

CONSCIENCE

The Still,
  Small Voice
Recoiling
  Recalling
Past misdeeds
  So far behind
Reflects...
      Resounds
On inner walls
    Of contemplating soul
Until it reaches
Decibels
      Uncomfortably
Disquietingly
      LOUD!

EVEN THE ROCKS HAVE TEARS

Even the rocks have tears
  When the sea wets them
And seagulls cry
  In the winds
Camouflaged by the mist
  Give birth in

The inexorable
  Passion of nature
Slow snails slide
  In awkward caress of

White pebbled sands
  Strewn with musky beach towels

Spread by frolicking people
  Throwing air-filled beach balls

And boisterous shouts that
  Deny the end

Even the rocks
  Have tears!

QUEST FOR EMPATHY

Humankind's quest for empathy
Asks no more
Demands no less
A resolute effort at
Unhesitating
Unblemished
Honesty
It seeks reprieve
From the
Sucking quagmire of
Conscious or unconscious
Blundering of
Half-truths
Lies disguised
Lies denied
It is striving for
Final
Eternal
Infinite Cosmic Awareness
Which survives
The Dim-Illusion
Death

NOT ENOUGH ALONE

Not enough alone
To wonder
    Where or
       What or
         Why
I am or
    Where I'm going
Empty
    As the sky that
       Clings like me
To some other ocean
    Beyond distant horizons
I cannot see
    Filled with uncertainty
Like unknown and
    Everchanging troughs
Upon the sea of life's experience
Touched by everyone's
    Salt spray air of
       Need
Pulled by
    The strength that to its
Bosom holds
    The tide
Like each wave to
    Some certain and
       Ephemeral destiny
As inevitable and
    Unrelenting as the tide
There is a destiny

As sure as every wave's demise
A certain
   Fated drop
    Within the
Oceans to rise

ALONE AND INDIFFERENT

I am alone
In my thoughts
In my world

Indifferent to the
Lives around me
Content in that indifference

Sated by the
Intertwining, impersonal
Contacts of the day

Yet alert in that indifference
To people
In my past

Mellow
In anticipation of
Things to come

Indifferent even to
The anxieties that tomorrow's
Speculations bring

Sad perhaps of
Too infrequent journeys
Into poem

Accepting of whatever
Life will bring
To penetrate this

Self-protective
Shield of
Indifference moved to sing of
Hope, Optimism, and Joy!

CROWDS

Crowds have
    Many faces
Though
    Many without names
Many sounds but often
    Abandon 'reason'
Crowds are
    Isolation cells for
      Lonely people
Whenever I want to be alone
    I join a crowd
And as ever adaptable man
    Will end in a shroud

THE PAINTER'S PALETTE

Colors evoke a powerful
Spectrum of Emotions
Moods, Sensations
Images
Like Joseph's coat of many colors
And the rainbow's arc

Inspiring the Painter's Palette
Colors from
White to black
Light to dark
Day to night
Warm to cool
Vibrant or quiet
Intense or subdued
Pure or mixed to add
Shading, tinting or hue

All the emotions and sensations
We can bear
Anger to ecstasy and joy
Depression to euphoria
Bitter to sweet
Ambivalence to certitude

White so pure
Reflects not
Colors back
Chaste, clean, virtuous
Guiding light

Seeking life force, 'Prana'
Blinding light
Pure love proclaims
Whitewash – clean!
Careful of the backwash
When you look the other way

Passionate Powerful Red
A color with heart
Vital and sexual
Energy at our core
Red carpets for VIPs
Cardinals elect a Pope
With a solemn puff of smoke
Red for Love or
Anger in its turn
Fight or flight
Stop at the light!

Toasty Amber, ill at ease
Optimistic and courageous
Energy and fire of the spirit
Talisman of beauty
Protection and renewal
Cautious in the middle
Careful of each
Next step to take

Fertile Healing Green
Growth and harmony at our root
Senses a tender touch
Greenlight – Go!

Sky's the limit
Envy and Jealousy
Take their turn
Puffed up with
Angry red

Juicy Optimistic Orange
Stimulating and emotive
Desire and procreation
Compassion
Adventure and risk-taking
Exciting and inviting
Harvest joy or
Grief for things or
Seasons past
Sacral near our core

Yellow… Stimulating or Mellow
Illuminating, uplifting, bright
Energy vortex fires up the night
Sunflowers and Daffodils despite
Traffic signs and
Taxis barely in our sight
Canary sentries in a mine
Cowardice more frequent than we care
Thinker not a Dreamer
Introspection and perfection
Confidence in its sight
Happy, cheerful, fun
Anxiety! – Beware!

Glittering Gold
　　Wealth, extravagance
　　　Wisdom, prestige
　　　　Power of the sun
　　Draws attention to itself
　　　Magnetic, optimistic, charismatic
　　　　High expectations and desires
　　Performance at its peak
　　　Stirs envy, even greed
　　　It's told

Silver, Sleek and Luxurious
　　Sparkling in jewelry
　　　Spiritual and silver-tongued
　　　　Intuitive and insightful
　　　　Moon and tides
　　　　Will come
　　Radiant and reflective
　　　Sophisticated, dignified
　　　　Seniors wear its wisdom
　　Sometimes second best

Earthy, Rustic Brown
　　Hides dirt within
　　　Sturdy, industrious
　　Comfortable
　　　Savory chocolate treats
　　Reliable
　　　Feet planted firmly on the ground

Pulsing Pomegranate
　　Bitter in color

Bitter in taste
Beigey orange of skin
Crimson red in seed
Puckers up the palette
Nutritious though indeed
Love, life, vitality
Success and power
Sin and destruction
In obverse

Serene and Confident in Blue
Water and sky
Carried on a Bluebird's back
Blue Spanish eyes entrance
Excitement and repose
Calming comfort
Inspires faith
Security and trust
Expressive and artistic
True voice emitted from the throat
Sometimes days are blue
Emoting sadness too

Luxurious Royal Purple
Creative and mysterious
Crown of life
Consciousness, spirituality
Transcendence
Awareness heightened
Arrogance on par
Decadence at worst

New Age Indigo
  Integrity, sincerity
    Meditative, introspective
      Opens up the mind
  Telepathic
    Charismatic
      Deep in thought
  Third eye on our brow

Transformative Magenta
  Harmony and balance
    Peace and inner calm
      Uplifting and compassionate
  Free spirit
    Not to be contained
  Careful of obsession
    Maintain an even keel

Loving Lavender
  Spring romance, nostalgia
    Calm and tranquil
      Creative spark
    Healing and anointing
      Secret garden, paradise
  Sensual in its dark

Sea's Garden Coral
  Medusa's blood did tint
    Tendrils like Medusa's hair
      Rise to seek the light
  Fertile
  Truthteller

> Protects from
> > Evil and our selves

> Tranquility in Pink
> > Caring in its warmth
> > > Elegant and mysterious
> > > > Exciting Eros
> > > > > Between our thighs
> > > > Arousing blissful sighs

> Pink again, now Tender
> > Feminine appeal
> > > Breath of
> > > > Intimacy and Love
> > Tossed about
> > > Like feathers on
> > > > Angel's wings
> > To capture in our hearts

> Gloomy Gray
> > Drizzly and ambiguous
> > > Conservative and reliable
> > > > Color of compromise
> > > > > And depression
> > Forebodes a peek
> > Beyond the veil
> Between this life
> And next

> Bold Judicial Black
> > Power and prestige
> > > Stretch limos and black ties

Elude the masses
Menacing, funereal in the dark
Vortex in outer space
Cloaks future from our eyes
Darkness 'seams' evil into
Its sinister disguise
Promises

A glimpse of
Dante's view of hell

FOOD FOR THOUGHT

"We either make ourselves miserable, or we make ourselves strong. The amount of work is the same." [3] Carlos Castaneda

"Friendship is a rainbow between two hearts sharing seven different colors: Secrets, truth, sadness, faith, happiness, respect, and love." Author unknown

"Colors, like features, follow the changes of the emotions." [4] Pablo Picasso

"Emotions are the colors of the soul." [5] William P. Young

"Happiness is like a butterfly; the more you chase it, the more it will elude you. But if you turn your attention to other things, it will come and sit softly on your shoulder." [6] Author Unknown

"The opposite of love is not hate, it's indifference." [7] Elie Wiesel

"And indifference is the opposite of both." Mel's corollary

"I dream my painting and I paint my dream." [8] Vincent van Gogh

CHAPTER 6
GIFTS OF NATURE

There is little so inspiring and emotionally uplifting as connecting with the beauty of 'Mother Earth' and the bounties of nature. This chapter deals with nature in many forms and the manner that we perceive and receive nature's overwhelming blessings. The chapter progresses through the many seasons and my experiences as I walked through life, whether in remote rural settings or in urban sprawl. Some of these poems also uncover anxieties that I have felt as I reflected on the future of this wonderful planet. Perhaps the reading of these poems will evoke similar feelings in you.

> *"The mountains are my bones,*
> *The rivers are my veins.*
> *The forests are my thoughts,*
> *And the stars are my dreams.*
> *The ocean is my heart,*
> *Its pounding is my pulse.*
> *The sounds of the earth write*
> *The music of my soul."* [1] Author Unknown

SEASONS

The vernal blanket
  Covering earth
    Fading in the sun
Will turn to autumn colors
  Loved by everyone
The reddish-orange and waxy yellow
  Soon turn to compost brown
Now lifeless leaves
  Reluctantly depart
    Their summer homes
In the breeze that beckons
  They flutter to the ground
In crispy mounds
  They huddle close
    To fend off winter chills
On streams, they drift
  Like vagrant boats
On aimless journeys to
  Forever lands

SUNRISE SIXTY-EIGHT

I love the shadows
Made at dawn
By a slumbering house
On a dew-drop lawn

The coldness, crispness
Freshness though
Of springtime mornings
With a summer glow

The distant hills
So peacefully
Awake and stir
Contentedly

I love the fields of
Sprouting grain
Absorbing from above
The sweet caress of
Sunray Love

While in peaceful meadows
Fresh in bloom
Cattle graze

Awaiting doom!

MID-DAY SUN

The mid-day Sun
     Begins to fall
From blue-illusion sky
Descending slowly
     In its path
To yawn
     Not yet to die
In cities men
     Their senses dazed
See only this
     Grey-purple haze

Shadows grow encompassing
     To ease the sun
          Into its bed
Their yellow glow
     To crimson turns
          Then puts them in their bed
The evening
     Dusk appears straight way
To aid the sun
     Star-cover lay
But with it
     Sun has taken
A distant, flickering beauty
     Now hidden from our eyes
Until again
ENCORE!
     SUNRISE!

MIDNIGHT WALK

A midnight walk or
  Solitary ride
Escaping human talk
  Bathing in evening light
Sensing nature's
  Pride
A mist in dreams
  With lovers' schemes
And now it seems
  Man's lost his way...
The love that helped
  To open up the day

CITY AT NIGHT

Midnight walks
    Round city blocks
Autumn fashion
    In quiet passion
Night lights on
    Peopled houses
Slow shadows linger
    Tease and kiss
Cold cement walks
    Tree-lined streets
        Rain-spattered breeze
Even the small
    Trees are majestic
        If you get under them
Think about how the trees
    Feel about the sky
Two blocks. A car.
    Alone
        Another motor's drone
Crickets chirping
    Deep within the silence
Lawns carefully placed
    To gently cushion
    The Fall of
Multi-colored leaves
    Cradle them in
        Winter's sleep
Running feet of a
    Love not yet satisfied
Silent lovers on

A midnight walk
Where even
Silence talks

BUFFALO POUND (1968 NEAR MOOSE JAW, SASKATCHEWAN)

Eastern dam
   A vast expanse of
      Captive water
   Long grass and reeds
      Marshy acres where
   The dike's inadequacy
   Overflowed

The hoarse call of
   Mating geese
      On flighty wings

Ducks plummeting
   To a watery landing

A gilded Teal
   A fledgling Heron
      On awkward limbs
   A Meadowlark
      A Whippoorwill

Sweet breeze caressing
   Gentle doe
      Knee-deep in swamp
   Gazing intently at

Shadowy rider
   Perched contentedly on
      Looming horse

High on a distant hill

LAKE ALMA (NEAR WEYBURN, SASKATCHEWAN 1969)

People are born here
    People die
Some live scarcely more
    Than a shadow existence

    Mere
    Spectres

Tossed about
    In the speechless winds and
      Drifting sands that
        Sweep across
      The uneasy, lonely
        Beauty
    Of

Lake Alma hills

THE HILLS ARE MINE

The hills are mine to walk
Alone from early dawn

Till dusk begins to
Slow the pace of day

Tufts of grass
Sand, red shale, clay

Miles and miles of
Nature's vast
Restless expanse

Silence broken by
Crickets, frogs, birds in
Nature's harmony

A soothing background for
Horizon falling
Upon horizon

Alone I see the hills
As they really are

Though I sometimes wonder
If just maybe

It's the you in me
That really sees

MEDITATIVE SPACE

Daphne, Mia Adora
Meditative space
Born, created
Out of soil
Nurtured by your
Labor of love
Mystical collusion
Harmonizing with
Nature
Smells of damp
Grass, ferns
Trees and leaves
Scents of Thyme, Fennel
Honeysuckle, Lavender
Daphne Odora
Leaves of Bay
From Laurel trees
Wafts of Cedar
Pitch of Pine
Eucalyptus, honeybees
Ocean smells
Drift up on
Gentle breezes
Infuse your space
Atop Cordova Bay
Melodies of birds
Little and large
Intermingling sensations
Excite then calm
Your senses

Bring joy
Restore, replenish
Make you whole

POINT NO POINT: A BIRTHDAY GIFT FOR LOVERS *

Land fingers
Projecting into
Strait of Juan de Fuca's
Saline seas
Point viewed from west
No point seen
Approaching from the east

Spindly sentinel Spruce
Branches extending open arms
In welcome
Fantail needles drooping
Languidly to rocks below
Yellow lichen on
Eastward flanks
Frame like pictures
The not-to-distant U.S. shore

Ships with cargo
Chugging heavy loads
Cruise ships
Edge along the coast to
Brave new worlds explore
Ripples barely noticed
On swells of
This vast expanse of water

Fishing charters and commercial
Set sail from Sooke
Along the shore

POETIC REFLECTIONS ON LIFE, LOVE AND PASSION   ·   145

Slow Salmon trawlers
Crabbers grabbing traps
Waves of calming rollers
Lap gently on the rocks
And soft contours of our minds

Heavy breakers on
Roller coaster rides
Roar against the shore
Roiling up the waters
Splashing salt spray in the air
Seaweed, flotsam, foam
Rise and fall
Moved by mighty oceans

We watch from fireplace
Deck or hot tub
Breathing in the
Wonder and the awe
Gulls and other seabirds
Chatter in the wind

While
Keenest kelp to shore
Come dragging vines of more
Seaweed dressed down in
Darkest green
Float in and out
With ebb and flow of
Fickle waves and whirlpools

Nearby a height of
Haughty Hemlock in
Respectful deference
Tip top hats to the east
And like seductive sirens
Invite to
Quick-end tea
Drink me, drink me
Drink me

* Point no Point resort
Northwest of Victoria and Sooke B.C.

SEA SWELLS

The sea frightens me
Unknown graveyard of
Countless ages
Dumping ground of
    Civilizations
Salty placenta
Aborting an
Undernourished
    Earth
The sea swells up
Within me
Crests and
    Falls of
Ages and
    Eons past and
Yet to come

SUMMER SCENES

Tampax tampons
    Buoyant pontoons
Crystal lakes
    White sand shores
Sunburnt backs
    Guilty snores
Sandcastle boys
    Ice-cream girls
Deep-sea searches
    Reluctant pearls
Hot dog stands
    Bikini sands *
The clock of life
    Reducing strands
That bind men to
    This earthly strife

*Bikini Atol, Marshall Islands site of 23 U.S. test nuclear explosions 1946-1958

SUMMER GONE

The Orange Globe of
>*Sunset in*
Patterned cloud fingers
>*Of streaking gray*
Penetrating to
>*Esthetic sensitivity*
In a cool
>*Mid-western night*
Slow autumn dance
>*Betrays the*
Beauty of
>*Summer Gone*
Subtly hints at
>*Birth of*
Winter's dawn

SNOWFLAKES

Snowflakes float
Whimsically upon the wind
   Drift
      Soar
         Fall
   Gentle merging of
      Terrestrial elements
Seeking
   Cosmic order
      Patterned perfection
Children frolic with Frosty
   Making snowmen
      Snow angels
Snowflakes melt
   Swept aside by
Busy wipers on
   Sliding cars on
      Slippery roads
With dizzy drivers
   Seeking stars and
      Sparkling moonbeams
On lonely roads
   In lonely lives
Where snowflakes fall

BOUGHS OF HOLLY

I cannot speak
The way I feel
For I am tied
To the golden wheel

Which turns and churns
It's golden round
Tracing life with
Ne'er a sound

While lowly man
With heart in hand
Succumbs, submits

In patterned folly
To love of God and
Boughs of holly

FOOD FOR THOUGHT

"Humankind has not woven the web of life. We are but one thread within it. Whatever we do to the web, we do to ourselves. All things are bound together. All things connect. We inherit the earth from our ancestors, and we borrow it from our children." [2] Chief Seattle

CHAPTER 7
HOPE AND INSPIRATION

This chapter begins with inspirational and insightful expressions of hope. It closes in the same fashion with multiple similar inspirational messages in 'Food for Thought. It traces the origin of the concept of hope in Greek Mythology, followed by a series of my own poems. Most are hopeful, except 'Creative Spark' which begins with the vitality of creativity, then mourns its loss.

"NOBODY can go back and start a new BEGINNING
But ANYONE can start today and make a new ENDING"
[1] Maria Robinson

"Hold fast to dreams, for if dreams die, Life is a broken-winged bird, that cannot fly."
[2] Langston Hughes

"It is only with the heart that one can see rightly;
what is essential is invisible to the eye."

[3] Antoine de Saint-Exupéry

"The flower that blooms in adversity is the rarest
and most beautiful of all." [4] <u>Mulan</u>

PANDORA'S BOX

Hope is vital to elevate the human spirit, to support dreams of the future, and give purpose and vitality to life.

In Greek Mythology, the god Prometheus stole fire from heaven to give to the human race, which originally consisted only of men. To punish humanity, the other gods created the first woman, the beautiful Pandora.

As a gift, Zeus gave her a box, which she was told never to open. However, as soon as he was out of sight, she took off the lid, and out swarmed all the troubles of the world, never to be contained.

Only Hope was left in the box, stuck under the lid. Anything that looks ordinary but may produce unpredictable harmful results can thus be called a Pandora's box. Merriam- Webster' Collegiate Dictionary

CREATIVE SPARK

Bright flame to
    Fading ember
Reservoir of
    Creative joy
Now depleted
    Brings the
Dim
    Dismaying
Emptiness of
    Effete creativity
Disheartens
    Disenchants
The migrant
    Soul of Striving
Artistry

COURAGE TO HEAL

Courage will outlast
   Most shadows of the past
Expose dark
   To light
Chase dark
   Away
      It will not last
A future
   Less troubled
Can come to you
   But you must
      Let out
The demons of the past
   You'll find new life
      A never easy path
Each step through this
   May be
      More painful than the last
But in the end
   You'll heal
      With new
Hope and expectations
   More realistic
      Than before
More steadfast
   Confident
      Less wary
Of how the future will unfold
You'll find new
   Love to cherish

A kind that
   Gives you HOPE
      For a better place to be
If you play the music stronger
   It will become
A SYMPHONY!

STRANGERS IN THE DARK

Don't be afraid
*   To smile at*
*   Strangers in the Dark*
Most of them are
*   A lot like you*
Wondering what you're like
*   Wondering what threat*
*   You might pose*
Uneasy
*   Maybe a little afraid*
*   You might do the unexpected*
Let down your guard and
*   Smile*
Smile at
*   Strangers in the dark*

TURNING POINTS

Saskatoon 1967
    House party
        I was enthralled
We somehow connected
    In a way that seemed unique
        Experienced by few
But you pushed me away
    In favor of another
        More than one of us
        On a string
In the meantime
    We pursued
        Other instincts of lust or love
My memory fades between then and
    1968 when you were somewhere
        Fending off bears and
I was elsewhere
    Writing poetry
        Exchanging love letters
Your visit to me there
    Taking you to your childhood home
        Highway hypnosis on my return
            Inspired yet another poem
You were my first love
    In retrospect, maybe I was yours
        But you didn't know it at the time
You had another
    Itch to scratch
Then saw me slip away
    Reached out to save US

To save me from uncertain future
Too late!
    I was ensnared
            Captivated
By another's eyes
We went our separate ways
        Our paths crossed intermittently from then
You had a child in wedlock
        With your other man
Then met another, remarried
        A rich life of travel
                Living overseas
Between '98 to now, arm in arm
        We walked the beach
                On a quiet ocean bay
                And other parks along the way
Will you stay
        Another night?
I could not
        That would have
                Changed everything
I followed your Facebook posts
        As my wife's health began to fail
In 2018 we reconnected
        You seemed to have a
Contented life BUT
        Accordionista, was there a
                Missing piece?
You were saturated
        But not overwhelmed
You sought to reconnect but
        Ambivalence seemed to

Intrude

    Make you wary

Which would it be?

    Revival of love or

        Maybe lovers?

Committed to deep exploration of

    What each of us became

With hindsight, insights and

    Enduring connections

A special place and time to

    Fill the empty spaces

Within us

    That no one else could do?

THE LOST FOREVER

The lost Forever
           Meets us   now
                     Upon the rivers
Of our minds
           Meeting
                     Fleeting
Phantasmal   Sparkle
                     Of
Elusive
                     Quintessential
Cosmic
           Jewel
                     Escaping
Vaping
                     Into
                          The
Infinite Depths
           The
Inner reaches
           Of
A Universal
           Unconscious

TROUBLED WATERS TROUBLED MINDS

Some people search
All their lives
Never find the water falling
Just the way
They want
Gently on the
Slow waves of
Troubled minds
They miss the soothing
Though sometimes irritating
Sound of a
Cricket night or
Eager neigh of
Scrambling colts
Waterfall and
Pot of gold at
Rainbow's End
Quiet
Soulful moments
Inhaling sometimes
Secret scents
That might precede
Feeling
SURPRISED BY JOY!

SOUL SEARCHING

I peered into
  Another's soul
Saw her darkness
  Saw her light
Saw her eyes
  Sparkle bright
Saw her ups
  Saw her downs
Saw her wrinkles
  Saw her frowns
Offered help, a
  Journey to complete
Take my hand
  Walk with me
We'll find a path
  Lit by fireflies
Follow fluttering butterflies
  Fretful faeries
Angels on
  Luminescent wings
Together we'll chase
  The darkness out
Your life whole
  Mine as well
Two journeys
  As one
Two lives fulfilled
Two lives now whole
Two lives complete

RAINBOW'S END

I've walked
  Many a mile
Since every Rainbow's End
  Was just a wish away
Every pot of gold
  Has stayed a wish ahead
I've walked
  Many a mile
Through smoke-filled haze
  And alcoholic daze
Melody now gone
  From lonesome cities
I took no time
  To listen then
Now I'll sit a while
  By the Banyan Tree
Draw its cosmic force
  Replenish my spirit
    My energy
Journey on
  Find hope at
    The
    Rainbow's End

FOOTPRINTS IN THE SAND [5] MARY STEVENSON

This poem has been an inspiration for me and millions of others. It reflects her faith. In her own words:

"I noticed that during the saddest and most troublesome times of my life, there was only one set of footprints. I don't understand why, when I needed You the most, You would leave me?

He whispered, "My precious child, I love you and will never leave you Never, ever, during your trials and testing!
When you saw only one set of footprints,
It was then that I carried you."

FOOD FOR THOUGHT –
WORDS OF INSPIRATION

"There are Three Lenses Through Which I View Life:
To Be
Optimistic and Disappointed for a Good Part of Your Life;
Pessimistic and Never Embark on Any Enterprise or Set Your Hand
to Anything;
Optimistic in Action, Pessimistic in Expectation, and Seldom
Anything but Pleasantly Surprised.

'Being Alone with Oneself Is the Depth of Despair;
Being Alone with the Universe is the Pinnacle of Ecstasy.

'The Road to Empathy Is a Void which Is
Traveled with the Greatest Adversity to the Human Ego;
The Greatest Blessing for the Human Soul."

Mel Gill (1945-)

"My past has not defined me
Destroyed me
Deterred me
Nor defeated me
It has only strengthened me.

'Your greatest self has
Been waiting your whole life;
Don't make it wait any longer.

'Your Dreams are
A poetic reflection of
Your soul's wishes.

Be courageous enough
To follow them.
'Let your past be
Your springboard
Not your quicksand."

[5] Dr. Steve Maraboli

Serenity Prayer
"God grant me the courage to
accept the things I cannot change
to change the things that I can and
the wisdom to know the difference."

Reinhold Niebuhr, AA

"There is no failure, except in no longer trying;
no defeat, except from within;
no insurmountable barrier,
except our own inherent weakness of purpose."

[6] Frank Hubbard

"The pessimist complains about the wind;
the optimist expects it to change;
the realist adjusts the sails."

[7] William Arthur Ward

"If you find yourself in a hole, stop digging."

[8] Will Rogers

"Creativity requires the courage to let go of certainties"

[9] Eric Fromm

"Darkness cannot drive out darkness,
only light can do that.
Hate cannot drive out hate,
only love can do that.
'Out of a mountain of despair,
A stone of hope."

[10] Martin Luther King Jr.

CHAPTER 8
LIFE'S LITTLE LESSONS

Explored in this chapter are some of the things that may dampen hope These poems challenge us to live in the present and strive to improve our lives. The experiences of living offer the opportunity to learn from our own successes, and failures. If we pay careful attention, learn from these and the wisdom of others, it can be of enormous benefit. Some of the 'truths' garnered from these experiences are captured in the wisdom of ages. This chapter ends with sage advice from others who share insights from experience.

"Wonder is the beginning of wisdom."

[1] Socrates

"Good judgment comes from experience,
and a lot of that comes from bad judgment."

[2] Will Rogers

"When in doubt, tell the truth."

[3] Mark Twain

*"No man ever steps in
the same river twice, for it's
not the same river and
he's not the same man."*

[4] Heraclitus

FRUITLESS SEARCH FOR WHY

Mankind's exasperation
  In fruitless
Thankless preoccupation

Is a well-spring of
  Neurosis and
Mental halitosis

Life – lived – well
  In meaningless devotion to
    Vacant
    Non-vocation

No longer
  Serves him well

Evolution's stronger child
  Has fathered

Man's indulgence in
  The happy hippy high

And absent-minded ply
  With the ever-present, nigh

LIVING IN THE MOMENT

It's foolish for people to
    Ignore lessons from the past
      There is no 'redo'
Foolish also to
    Worry about the future since
It is a world which we of
    The present will never inhabit
If we focus on the present
    The future will take care of itself
If we become obsessed
    With either
Even the present
    Will escape us
What is the future or past
    Without THIS moment
Lived intensely in the present

LIFE'S INJUSTICES

The world as mass production
   Ejecting
      Paranoid schizophrenics
      Manic Depressives
A burning incense world of
   Psychopathic success stories
'CERTIFIED' by
   Governmental 'green'
Superego self-importance
   The RAW injustice of
      Social immobility
Propagating in kind
Bringing
   Justice and Idealism to
A Cruel and
   Devastating
      DEMISE

COMPLEX WORLD

Images in my mind
*   Flash painful visages*
Spun from a nagging
*   Anxiety in a*
Turbulent
*   Too large*
Too complex
*   World*
Ignorance, poverty [5]
*   Gender, income, other inequalities*
Distrust bred by
*   Impersonal distance*
Between strangers too
*   Fearful of what might come*
From chance encounters in this
*   'Brave New World'* [6]

"The comfort of the rich depends
upon an abundance of the poor."

[5] The American Ruling Class

[6] Aldous Huxley

I USED TO DREAM

I used to Dream
Hours and hours
Days and nights
When the stars
Took off the cloaks
That covered up
Their brights
I used to Dream of
Astronauts
Spaceships
Drifting through
Galaxies
Exploring
New domains
THAT WAS IN MY YOUTH
Now all that
Remains
Contemplation
Procreation
Life's salvation
The Sleep of Death

WORDS BENT TO CONFUSE

Words Bent to
Confuse
The mind
Like amorphous manipulations
By some unseen hand
The anguish and agony of
Some superior
Intellectual
Pandora's box
Opened with so many
Different handles
Windows seen through
Reflecting back
Images, imaginings of
The Seer
False prophets among
Prophets false foretelling
Future fantasies
Facts
Which
Only time
Frozen in a single instant
Will ever prove or
Put the lie to
Is the parable proof
Of a much larger

TRUTH

BETRAYALS

What is this word, betrayals?
How did it come to be?
Is it simply something less
Than you expected?
Did your hopes and your desires
Fall short of all your aspires?
Did others fail their duty
To protect you?
Did the trust you put in
Someone fail you?
Have you suffered grave
Abuse?
Did someone close
Back-stab you?
Was your loyalty
Unrequited?
Was contract breached or
Just misunderstanding?
Did a lover's indiscretion
Distress you to the core?
Does your object of affection
Now love you less or more?
Did secrets kept
Destroy you? Or
Surprise with
Joy and excitation?
Was concealment
Worse than truth?
What cost to hide it
Even from yourself?

Speak your truth, but speak with care
The truth can set you free!
But there is
No guarantee!

"Three things cannot long stay hidden:
the sun, the moon, and the truth." [7] Gautama Siddhartha

FOOD FOR THOUGHT

"I only went out for a walk
And finally concluded
To stay out till sundown
For going out I found
Was really going in"
[8] John Muir

"The words of truth are always paradoxical." [9] Lao Tsu

'Once I let go of who I am, I can become who I might be." [9] Lao Tsu

"It is better to keep your mouth shut and appear stupid than to open it and remove all doubt." [10] Mark Twain

"Some people drink from the fountain of knowledge. Others just gargle." [11] Robert Anthony

"Good judgment comes from experience, and a lot of that comes from bad judgment." [12] Will Rogers

"Life is not always a matter of holding good cards, but sometimes, playing a poor hand well." [13] Jack London

"I have lived in this world just long enough to look carefully the second time into things that I am most certain of the first time." [14] Josh Billings

'It's not so much the things you don't know that get you into trouble. It's the things you know, that just ain't so." [14] Josh Billings

"Science has proof without any certainty. Creationists have certainty without any proof." [15] Ashley Montague

"Religion is a culture of faith; science is a culture of doubt." [16] Richard Feynman

'The first principle is that you must not fool yourself--and you are the easiest person to fool." [16] Richard Feynman

"Absence of evidence is not evidence of absence." [17] Altman and Bland

"Every problem comes with a solution. If we keep staring at the problem, we fail to see the solution it has within." [18] Author Unknown

"You must correctly 'name' the problem or all your solutions will be incorrect." [19] Paulo Friere

'If your only tool is a hammer, then everything will look like a nail." [20] Abraham Maslow

"The world is not to be narrowed till it will go into the understanding, but the understanding is to be expanded till it can take in the world." [21] Sir Francis Bacon

CHAPTER 9
EXISTENTIAL MOMENTS

The chapter begins with reflections on the purpose of human existence and some of its stark realities. It closes with 'Food for Thought' which includes a brief essay on Peak Experiences and Transcendence. It is intended to stimulate reflection and soul-searching. The quotations have been mind-opening for me.

"In the ocean of pure awareness, on the surface of the universal consciousness, the numberless waves of the phenomenal worlds arise and subside without beginning or end. As consciousness, they are all me. As events they are all mine. There is a mysterious power that looks after them. That power is awareness, Self, Life, God, whatever name you give it."

[1] Nisargadatta Maharaj

"Most men lead lives of quiet desperation and go to the grave with the song still in them." [2] Henry David Thoreau

PURPOSE OF LIFE

Birth through Life, Living, Dying, and Death
We, humans, have only
A Brief Moment in Time
To find the Purpose and
Meaning of Life

Life itself may be a purpose of
A grander universal scheme

But the purpose of each of our own lives
Must be sought within ourselves
Living in the Moment
Our Moment and in Our Time
Our purpose is otherwise

Only a passing, transitory voyage
Through Darkness and Light
Loving yourself and others

Striving to do as much as you can
To make the world a better place
Than you entered and leave it
For Future Generations of

Humans and fellow travelers on this planet
Set your compass on your goal
Sail into Light
Find Anchor in

Safe harbor to
Protect from
Storms of Darkness

If life is worth living

It's only worth living together... connected
Together there's purpose
Alone we sail in darkness
If you will be my anchor
I will be your guide
Together we'll
Sail into
Eternity
Sayonara!

EGOLESS

Only the 'i' in 'I'
Is very real
It is the core of
Selflessness
The rest is
Just an illusion
Something we tell ourselves
To protect us
From what?
From insecurity
Lack of self-worth
From life
From recognition
Of ego's
Ultimate demise
A crutch
We lean on
To seek purpose and
Meaning for our lives
Why can't we be
Just 'i'

PATTERNS

From creation
  To salvation
So closely intertwined
  No one makes
      A sense of it

The world belches
Toxins and no one
Sees the pattern

Instincts of the mammal
Homo sapiens
Judged the 'wiser kind'?

Curiosity of
  Human minds

Plagued by
  Vacillation and anomie

Fall back to
  Simple
      Pro-
          Creation

With
  Nothing more
    In mind

EPIPHANY

The common face
A beauty trace,
Uncommon place

Time can't erase
Mental stirrings of
Mankind all

Silhouettes and
Vague recall

Conscious beckoning
Subconscious
Conscious

Reckoning and
All at once
The pattern sets
You know!

CRYSTAL CLEAR

What color is eight
  What color is two
What color is sex
  What color is blue
What color is love
  What color is hate
What color
    A cut-glass goblet
Is the vision clear?
    Enter
Tap of water
    A sink
        A splash
Down the drain
    A blob
        A million years now gone
A soiled white cloth
    The drops are dry
Glass to crystal
Years now crystal clear
    Yet
I know not
    What they mean!

SUICIDE

No one
> *Nothing*
>> *Alone*
So goddamn lonely
The telephone
> *Not that place again*
No. God damn it!
> *Oh, God!*
What?
> *The sink?*
>> *Blood?*
My God....
> *Quick...stop.... STOP IT!*
Who?
Oh............ you?
> *Too late!*

HOUSE PARTY

A good time might have been had!

Midsummer night
    Suburban pool
        Private fence flags of
        Silent ash

Alone on red brick walk
    A pair of thongs
        Stands
            Empty now

Cool breeze begins
    To rustle leaves

A doorknob turns
    Inside the swell of
        Merriment rings

A female giggle
    Tinkling glass
        Click
            A gasp

A body bobs
    Ghastly grin on
        Drowned drunk face

A terror-stricken
    SCREAM!

IMPRINTS OF CULTURE

Night and Day
Are here to stay

The seasons change
Come what may

The human mind
Wills ne'er to sway

From imprints of culture
Made day by day

IF NOT NOW

Life
Barely a
Spark
In
Time
Flashed past
Brief memories
Soon forgotten
Promises made
To ourselves
Loves
The world
Still unfilled
New year's
Resolutions
Barely edited
From year to year
Promises
That take
A moment
To make
A lifetime
To honor
As the
Inevitable
End
At accelerating
Pace
Draws
To a slow or

Painful
Abrupt
Cessation
Promises?
If not
Now,
When?

RULER OF THE SKIES

Majestic Eagle
Ruler of the skies
Eagle feathers adorn
Totem Spirit Guide

Sharp eagle eyes
Laser focus from high
Awesome in vision
Wondrous in sight
Magnificent in flight

In freedom it soars
On Wingspans eight feet
Glides through the clouds
Knows when to coast
To go with the flow
And when to let go
Lightning-like flash! as it
Dives for its quarry

Hooked beaks and claws
Pierce, rip and tear
Bring panic and fear to
Feast of the day
Wrist tendons lock
Onto its prey
Clasping till death

Strength of purpose
Courage and wisdom
Spiritual protector...
Healer illuminates
Once hidden truths.

Bearer of life
Rendering death
Rebirth and renewal
Symbol of cultures
Values and times

Transcends motifs of
Nations and flags
Mystical in meanings
Messenger of gods.

Visit in Parksville
Wonderful friends
Eagle ascendant in
Both of our lives

Out on the deck
Gliding above
A welcoming kettle
Eagles galore!
More than a score!
Lower than treetops!
Accepted as blessing
Our love now renewed

Short weeks later
Up Island again
Alone this time
Weakened in breath
More magic mine
An eagle did call
Where are you?
I quietly asked.

One glorious eagle flew
Out and away
Alighted on treetop
Land point afar
Joined another I'd
Not seen thus far

Next day another
Perched on post
Above water
No fish below

I wondered
Was this just for me?
To hear and to heal?
Spiritual guidance
Message for love

Momentous connection
Life yet to live
Love amplified
To strengthen

This union of souls
Intertwined
Separate < and > Interdependent
'Me'
Embraced within
'We'

Mel < and > Daphne
written in Daphne's voice

MILLENNIUM

The Human Species
  Will have
A brief moment
  A flicker in Eternity
An infinitesimally small flash
  Of Collective Consciousness
Searing insight
  Then
Blind Panic
  Cries of Anguish for
Opportunities missed
  Wrong choices
    Failed chances
Just before
  The END!

TRANSCENDENCE (BRIEF ESSAY)

A peak experience is a moment accompanied by a euphoric mental state often achieved by self-actualized individuals. The concept was originally developed by Abraham Maslow in 1964, who described peak experiences as "rare, exciting, oceanic, deeply moving, exhilarating, elevating experiences that generate an advanced form of perceived reality. They are even mystic and magical in their effect upon the individual."

There are several unique characteristics of a peak experience, but each element is perceived together in a holistic manner that creates the moment of reaching one's full potential. Peak experiences can range from simple activities to intense events; however, it is not necessarily about the activity, but the ecstatic, blissful feeling experienced during it.

Fresh air drafts in through open doors and minds. Peak experiences for me are...a sense of euphoria, peacefulness, lightness, ecstasy. C.S. Lewis called it being 'Surprised by Joy'.[3] C.S. Lewis

"The moments of happiness we enjoy take us by surprise. It is not that we seize them, but that they seize us." [4] Ashley Montague

AN EXPERIENCE OF JOY AND SORROW

I awakened early after a night of passionate love with a smile on my face, joy, and love in my heart. I was amazed at the reawakening of this love. Near ecstatic at the wonder of it all.

Then a darkness began to fall over me. I was overwhelmed with a profuse eruption of tears like geysers flooding my entire being. Images of sorrowful faces began to flash like a never-ending parade before my mind's eye. I could not stem the flow. Great sorrow and pain. Weeping and gnashing of teeth. Then swarms of black, evil creatures like bats or birds out of Hitchcock's movie, seemed to flow into Jesus on the cross, into his body and soul as though he was taking all the tribulations, pain, sorrow and sins of the world into his entire being in a cleansing of the world. Never ending tears and sadness continued as I watched this flow, like dark energy being sucked into the vortex of a black hole.

I was transformed in fundamental ways to the core of my soul and in ways I do not yet know! It was like a deep, festering sore had broken open releasing all the anguish, pain and darkness that had weighed me down over the years, releasing my own Pandora's box of evils. Yet along with that, some hope for love renewed. Stripped naked for all the world to see my solitary vulnerability, this experience gave way to new vitality and spring in my step. It gave me a new understanding of myself that seared into my mind and cleansed my soul.

FOOD FOR THOUGHT

"Your joy can fill you only as deeply as your sorrow has carved you." [5]
Kahlil Gibran

The lamp of the body is the eye. If therefore your eye is good, your whole body will be full of light. But if your eye is bad, your whole body will be full of darkness. If therefore the light that is in you is darkness, how great is that darkness!" [6] Bible

God or some other omnipotent universal force* should be able to create something out of nothing if matter is something and energy is nothing: e = mc². Mel Gill

*Psychic, spiritual, harmonious universal energy.

"There is a wound in every psyche, a portal that lets the dark and light get in and out. In the best of worlds, the light will chase the darkness out. An unattended wound will fester, sow dissonance and may grow to destroy you.' [7] Mel Gill (Adaptation from Rumi and Cohen)

"Someone I loved once gave me a box full of darkness. It took me years to understand that this too, was a gift." [8] Mary Oliver

"War does not determine who is right - only who is left." [9] Anonymous

"Only the dead have seen the end of war." [10] George Santayana

CHAPTER 10
GROWING OLD

I muse. What does life mean in this second last chapter of my journey? What joyful memories do I recall? What painful regrets and disappointments? What milestones do I celebrate? What do I feel and wonder about as I approach the end of this brief existence? What do others feel as they grow old? What anxieties do we hold in common?

PEOPLE, LONELY PEOPLE

People, Lonely People
Searching for life in
The uncertain flicker of
A dying candle
In the silent descent of
The night mantle
And in
The infinite nothingness
Between
People, Lonely People
Searching for the meaning of existence …
for the
Invisible thread that ties together generations
Grasping for each other and
In their blindness
Reaching past the plaintiff cry in
Each of us that says
Here am i, here am i
Your hand and love reached out to me
For this I thank you darling and
Thank your Mother too
Who long ago gave birth to you
Full unaware
Your birth
Gave birth to two

TIME

Time is the ticking of an Alarm** !!! Clock
In a Lonely Bedroom
It's waking up in the morning and
Looking in the mirror to find another
Grey hair which wasn't there the night before
It's waking up in the morning and fearing
You won't recognize the image that you see
Time is telling an old friend how much
she's changed
And hoping she'll remember you
Time is passing up a game or fishing trip for
An extra hour's sleep
It's sleeping in Sunday morning
Napping Sunday afternoon because
You didn't sleep enough the night before
Time is sitting back in your rocking chair and
Watching the children play on the floor
When yesterday you would have joined them
And the day before … they were you!
Time is the silence as your last breath says …
I'm ready!
And time is the alarm now silent to your ears
In that lonely bedroom you once slept, lived,
loved and
Hoped for peace, redemption and gra-
cious blessings
From a Master whose existence you ques-
tioned many times

SIXTIETH ANNIVERSARY

(MY PARENTS, HENRY AND EDNA GILL, 1989)

Not wedded bliss
    Though
        Love and
            Perseverance
In early years
    No limousines
Just long, long walks
    And buggy rides

Toil and struggle
    Pain and woe
To eke a
    Living with
        The hoe
Glaslyn years
    Depression times
    Relief enough to basics buy
    Breaking Land
    Back-breaking work
Henry cutting wood
    Fifty cents a cord
        Sometimes in hip-deep snow
Edna baking, canning, scrubbing
    Bare wooden floors

Yet through it all
    Some joy
        Some hope
A son

A war
    Another son

The Lerner farm
    Then their own
        And Leader bound

More struggles true
    Not quite so bad

The fifties,
    Though no jubilee
        Bountiful harvests
Awaiting verdict anxiously on
    Malting barley hopes
Grandchildren two
    Then two more
        Finally. Another

Year by year
    Arm in arm
Their paths
    Through life
        They wrought

Till sixty years
    A milestone

To which
    So few are
        Brought

MEMORIES

Remember when
You were young and gay and fancy-free
And didn't stop to think
   Just what would be
The consequence
   Of loving me
Remember when
You said you would
I replied
   Do you really think we should?
You said anyway
   You would
     And so, we did!
Remember when
   We lay in bed
You said you wished that you were dead
   And now you are
I still remember when
   And now it seems so far away
It doesn't matter anymore
   Soon not even I
     Will
Remember when

LAST FEW LINES

Someday I'll write
    A last few lines
That speak of
    Grief and
        Pain and
           Sorrow
That speak of
    Love and
        Strife and
          Joy
    Tomorrow

Lines the furrows in the
    Brow of life

A last few lines
    Before I'm free
        From the burdens of
This world
    And ME!

FOOD FOR THOUGHT

"It is not true that people stop pursuing dreams because they grow old, they grow old because they stop pursuing dreams." [1]
Gabriel García Márquez

"Just 'cause there's snow on the roof doesn't mean there's not fire inside."[2] Bonnie Hunt

"Age is an issue of mind over matter. If you don't mind, it doesn't matter." [3] Mark Twain

"Some people try to turn back their odometers. Not me; I want people to know why I look this way. I've traveled a long way, and some of the roads weren't paved.

"The older we get, the fewer things seem worth waiting in line for."
[4] Will Rogers

TRAIN OF THOUGHT (POSTED SIGN, AUTHOR UNKNOWN)

> *"I've Reached*
> *The Age Where*
> *My Train of Thought*
> *Often Leaves The*
> *Station*
> *Without Me"*

How to Stop Time

"How to stop time: kiss.
How to travel in time: read.
How to escape time: music.
How to feel time: write.
How to release time: breathe."

[5] Matt Haig

CHAPTER 11
DYING AND DEATH

The final chapter in life! A release for some. Quiet contemplation. Is there existence beyond this? Have I left the world a better place than when I entered? How do others experience this last chapter of life?

"Keep death always at your left hand." [1] Carlos Casteneda

"To die is poignantly bitter, but to die without having lived is unbearable." [2] Eric Fromm

"The idea is to die young, as late as possible." [3] Ashley Montague

"There are four questions of value in life, Don Octavio. What is sacred? Of what is the spirit made? What is worth living for and what is worth dying for? The answer to each is the same. Only love." [4] Lord Byron

"Let us endeavor so to live that when we come to die even the undertaker will be sorry." [5] Mark Twain

"One must wait until evening to see how splendid the day has been!" [6] Will Rogers

"Life and death are one thread, the same line viewed from different sides." [7] Lao Tzu

MORTAL SHACKLES

I do not like
  The mortal shackles

Which bind me to the
  Earthly tides
    That lap the world in

Generations of spineless
    Spiteful

Mortal man who
  Loves in lust
  And kills in spite
Lives and Lies to others
  Yet himself is not deceived

While the evolution of the
  Soul and humankind are grieved

I do not like the
  Mortal shackles that

Confine my mind
  Dim its scope

Restrict its knowledge
  Leave but hope

In uncertain life
More certain death in the

Wake of
Mortal shackles

COME QUICKLY DEATH

Come quickly
> *Death*

Enfold my body
> *Lying restless*

In dreams of
> *Tomorrows*
>> *That never came*

Spawned by yesterdays
> *That gave the dreams*
>> *Their life*

Come softly
> *Death*

Ensnare
> *My soul*
>> *My being*

Past tense
> *Whole!*

TRIBUTE TO A FRIEND

(ROY SCORY (DEC 15, 1946- MAR 11, 2018) LOYAL FRIEND, SPORTSMAN, RACONTEUR)

Roy, your friendship has been a Blessing for me, my family and the
Multitude of others who have shared your life in one way or another.
You have had more friends than anyone else I know, as well as
Mother, brothers, sister, wife who have loved you dearly.

Remember the refrain: "I can't get no Satisfaction, I tried and I tried"
One starry night when we were young. Well you tried, and
You had a generous share of Satisfaction. And you
Got it maintaining Integrity!

Your decision to end your life on your terms was Courageous
That's how you've always been! You walked to the
Threshold, hesitated a moment, and then caring hands
Drew you into the cold embrace

You were always there for me when I needed you
No matter the distance…which will be greater now than ever
Unless you can penetrate the Veil that will separate us.

So, the day is fast approaching. I hear the distant hoofbeats of
A Winged horse…Pegasus and ask…
Hey Roy, hey Roy is that your horse?
You smile enigmatically…
Not the time for quick wit and retorts,
which so
Endeared you to us.

You'll mount the steed and slowly drift off
In Winged Flight and Silent Hoofbeats

In search of the Happy Hunting Grounds
You've had a Good Ride with a loving
Soul Mate, Lorraine, as your partner on the journey

May you find Kay, Ruth, and Gary there
And if perchance you see Judith
Know she loved you too.

You will always live in our memories
Until we join you, as we surely will
Thank you for welcoming us into your family!
"You betcha!"

Love, Mel, Trent, and Joel

BOUQUET OF CARES

Everyone carries
  A bouquet of cares

Gathered and sorted
  Like roses from thorns

Held in suspension
  With smiles upon scorns

Everyone carries
  Their own special way

Dealing with problems
  That come day by day

No one is buried
  Alone in the grave

We all will be holding
  That bouquet of cares

"After the game, the king and the pawn go in the same box."

Italian Proverb

THE RUSSIANS ARE COMING
(DEATH OF DEMOCRACY, MAYBE 'CIVILIZATION')

Afghanistan 1979

Czechoslovakia 1968

Chechnya 1994 and 1997

Georgia 2008

Ukraine and Crimea 2014

Red armies

Rape with

Penetrable ease

Uncountable dead

Massive movements

Promised improvements

Communist leaders' aggressions

Ambitions appeased

FAST Forward

Cyber war, election interference

Rebukes superciliously dismissed

Hammer Sickle

Language Fickle

Treacherous lies

Straight-faced denials

Russian hackers

Fancy bear, cozy bear

REALLY!

Destroying democracies

Gucifer.2 more aptly named

'L' displaced

Putin unashamed

Many others blamed

Watch out for

China, Iran and more!

DEVIL'S LAUGHTER

The Shadows of
    The Night appear
To dance
        Hysterically!
Upon the graves
    Of 'Once-Begotten'
        Souls
That now lie
    Sleeping
        Dormant
            Covered
In cold black holes
    Or
Burnt to Ashes
    In momentary sojourn
        Through a Fiery Hell
Scattered to drift on the
    Winds
        Waters
        Dust
    Of
ETERNITY

LOSS OF A CHILD (WRITTEN FOR HELEN AND HARRISON MADIGAN IN MEMORY OF SON PATRICK KILLED IN A VEHICLE ACCIDENT IN 1991 NEAR RENFREW, ONTARIO)

Words can't replace
Nor time erase
The agony, the pain
The grief will wane
Though scars remain
Life never quite the same
The forever walk on
Tomorrow's road
More lonely will it be
With each new step
The burden lightens
Fond memories flash
Days do brighten

IMITATION ROSES

A womb portal opens
Painfully
Turbulently
Screams to face
The light of day
Cotton diapers
Flushabyes
A black lid closes
Softly on
Satin-pillowed head
Only
Imitation roses
In between

GRIEF'S PASSAGES

DEATH
    TRANSITORY
        OVERSHADOWING LIFE
For those who remain behind
    Unable
        To see beyond
            The impenetrable
VEIL
    That separates the quick
    From the cold and
        Unrelenting darkness or
Perhaps

A LIGHT We Cannot See
Which

SHROUDS
    The once active, precious, living
        Form that
            Gave us
                Held us
                    Loved us
                Laughed with us
                    Cried for us
                        Cried with us
SACRIFICED
    For us
        Again
            Again
                And once again

NOW GONE
  Body Buried or Burned
    Spirit Free
A wellspring of emotions
   Erupt!

DENIED at first
  It cannot be!
   Primal screams!
    Wailing and gnashing of teeth!
GRIEF
  Comes
   Slowly sometimes
    Sometimes with a rush
     Of uncontrollable
SOBS
  And tears
   Welling up from a reservoir
    Of hurt and
     Love and
      Guilt and
ANGER
  For the loss and, perhaps,
   For our own diminishing capacity or
    Indiscretions, misdeeds or betrayals
     Unchallenged
      Unrepented
       Unforgiven
RELIEF
  Perhaps
   From a burden of caregiving or
    Irreparable relationship

GRATITUDE
    For life and loves
      Shared times
        Shared memories

WE MOURN
    For parent
      Lineage
        Progeny
          Lovers
            And more
    And then!

EXISTENTIAL ANGST
    From the
      Fear of Death
        We each must face in
          The relentless march of the

COSMIC FORCE
    Collective Unconscious
      Universal Soul
      Which ties
        Each of us
TOGETHER
    With one another
      Generation to generation
        In
LOVE
    And hate
    In war and peace

Within

    Without

WORDS

    Of comfort

      In prose

        And poem

EXPUNGE

    The pain

      Slowly

        Slowly

          But never enough!

NEVER ENOUGH

    They deepen desire

      For one more

        Moment of

          Quiet!

            To recapture the

JOY

    A fleeting touch

      Soft caress

        Quiet word of kindness

      Tender smile

        Spark of laughter

      Gentle reproach

LONGING

    For one brief parting

      Of the Seamless Curtain

        That separates us

        Though not in thought

          Or Memory… creating

HOPE
    More than ever before
        For a glorious reunion
        Of which the
PROMISE
    Can only be seen
        If at all
            From the Other Side
        Of the
VEIL
    Where peace and serenity
        May know no bounds
        And only those
            Who have passed through

THIS SEAMLESS WEB
    Between life and death
        May discern at last

    Perhaps

It's MEANING
    MEANING?
        MEANING?
        MEANING?

DEATH WALK (JANUARY 17, 2018)

Ten days holding
        My true love's
                Hands
Just three hours
        Home to catch
                Some sleep
Phone call... ... ...
        Judith is no more
She died?
Primal screams
I was not there
        To hold her
                As she took her
Final breath
Rush to the hospital
        As though it could
                Reverse the course

NO CHANCE!

Staff condolences
Doctor Death
        Certificate
Lift the sheet
        To reveal her once beautiful
Face now frozen in time
        Our son lovingly closed
                Her once-enchanting eyes
        That now stared aimlessly
                Hauntingly etched in our memories

Need to dress her body
    Her body to embrace
They need to clean her first

    MORE

Tears and sobs we trace
Cremation service called
Two hours long we wait
Man and woman
    Dark eye-shadowed
        Like spectres closing lives
    NOW
Spirit soaring
    Free of pain
        So far's we know
She's wrapped in
    Pure white linen
Placed gently in a
Shroud of blue
    Bagged to go
On gurney
    Take the helm
Guide her to
    That final journey
Condolences again
    Eight months later... only now
Can I record that night!
Released from my own pain
    For now
    Perhaps to
Meet again

BENEDICTION FOR CAREGIVERS

May your life be Blessed in All Matters
Guided by Wisdom and Good Judgement
May your servitude to Standards and Policies be
Tempered by Common Sense and
Personal Accountability
May you carry The Golden Rule with you
Every Step of your own professional and per-
sonal journey
May the Light of the Universe Uplift you, Brighten
Lives and
Protect you from Darkness and Evil
May you have Peace, Integrity, Good Health,
Good Humor, Happiness, and
Occasionally be <u>Surprised by Joy!</u>

Mel and Judith Gill, Forever thankful 1968 to 2018

JUDITH'S EPITAPH

Let no one mourn me, for
i die not!

Rather, i cast off the fetters of
Consciousness and
Loose the locks that bind me
To this earth

I Pass

i drift unrehearsed into
The infinite reaches of galaxies
Unfettered by the specious present,
And drift phantasmally among the stars

Ethereal Essence Dancing
Seven Veils softly
Through luminescent clouds of
Jung's 'collective unconscious'
And de Chardin's 'noosphere'

i am part of the universal soul
Pure energy unleashed

No longer constrained by strictures
Imposed by obsequious obedience to

These Master Dimensions...
Time, Space, Gravity, Sound
Darkness, Light and Matter

Though I have 'mattered' to many...
And many to me!

Mel to Judith with Love!

BEQUEST

To the winds I bequeath
My Ashes
To my Friends
My Love
To Acquaintances
I leave the memories
To my enemies and detractors
I leave my empathy
To Humanity
The legacy of Hope
And
Aspirations of
The Spirit
Which I leave
For
INFINITY!

FOOD FOR THOUGHT

'Wrinkles are but Furrows on the Brow of Life." Mel Gill

"Truth forever on the scaffold, Wrong forever on the throne, Yet, that scaffold sways the future, and, behind the dim unknown, Standeth God within the shadow, keeping watch above his own." [8] James Russell Lowell

"I regard the brain as a computer which will stop working when its components fail. There is no heaven or afterlife for broken down computers; that is a fairy story for people afraid of the dark." [9] Stephen Hawking

"---common sense tells us that our existence is but a brief crack of light between two eternities of darkness... I have... groped for some secret outlet only to discover that the prison of time is spherical and without exits... I was unaware that time, so boundless at first blush, was a prison." [10] Vladimir Nabokov

I don't want my life to be defined by what is etched on a tombstone. I want it to be defined by what is etched in the lives and hearts of those I've touched." [11] Dr. Steve Maraboli

"And at the instant he knew, he ceased to know." [12] Jack London

"They work to pass, not to know, and outraged Science takes revenge. They do pass, and they don't know." [13] Aldous Huxley

"Death may be the greatest of all human blessings." [14] Socrates

The Indispensable Man [15] Saxon White Kessinger

Kessinger challenges our arrogance, egotism, and sense of self-importance with her own reflections in the following verse:

"Take a bucket and fill it with water
Put your hand in it up to the wrist
Pull it out, and the hole that's remaining
Is a measure of how you'll be missed"

"Age has no reality except in the physical world. The essence of a human being is resistant to the passage of time. Our inner lives are eternal, which is to say that our spirits remain as youthful and vigorous as when we were in full bloom. Think of love as a state of grace, not the means to anything, but the alpha and omega. An end in itself." [16] Gabriel García Márquez

ENDNOTE

AGE OF AQUARIUS

Feb. 15, 2018 – A new moon and a partial solar eclipse, both occurred at the same time.

"This day was a cosmic gift to remind us all of the endless cycles of nature. A day to reaffirm the need to shift our perspectives … swim in that contemplative place … and begin the process of letting go." [17] Gayle McDonald Globe and Mail, Feb. 15/18

AFTERWORD

Mel Gill's book of poems and reflections confronts and embraces one of the great paradoxes of art. At some point in Mel's career, the career of a poet who has a substantial body of work behind him, I imagine him sketching out his next work. He undertakes this task with the full knowledge that the words, phrases and stanzas of what he might write, in theme and execution, will contain the annihilation point of both the idea and the process. Simply put, Mel knows that his poems will contain the basic elements of their own destruction.

What does that mean? How does this come about, and to what value? Is the proposition a metaphorical allusion to a problem of aesthetics, or something else? Setting aside the implications of the title, Mel points toward an answer in <u>Chapter 10: Growing Old,</u> where he quotes a series of observations on how to 'control' time. The fourth of these is:

"How to feel time: write!"

This seems clear enough. Anyone who writes is familiar with the fact that the necessary mental work makes the perception of time drag horribly. And it does so to the point where, for most writers, all but the most utilitarian writing goes uncompleted back in the drawer. So there we have one death and can move to the second, which concerns the act of writing and its one guaranteed pleasure - the relief of finishing and being left the feeling of **having** written. And **having written** at least one poem, the erstwhile poet might well feel free from any further obligation to art. Perhaps forever. Another death of sorts.

But time passes and feelings change. Some writers might feel that the concept of 'having written' feeds more into the curiosity of 'what have I written?' They feel the desire to know what gems they once created. They might, like Mel, be aware that the mental energy of creating art, like the physical energy of fire, is transformed in the process but never lost; no small task to go find it. So, with fresh eyes and a hopeful attitude, Mel Gill, the writer, reads the words he had written years ago, maybe decades ago. But the thing he ponders are the images and ideas he sees **now**. And he's not a little surprised to notice that things have changed. The gems are there; but now they glow with deeper or different colors than those he originally devised. Moreover, the supporting ideas that once lifted the poem into the spotlight have now moved to a different vantage place, changing the focus into something more intense, more visceral, more personal. But the words haven't changed. So, it must be something in him, in the writer, who by experience, increased knowledge, the manifold influences of society has altered dramatically.

But in time, Mel changes. The experience of the years, the drag of time, the good and horrible episodes of living have in effect 'destroyed' his original work; at least his original thoughts about it. But the vital fire of wordsmithing, the energy expended over decades of life is not lost, only preserved in a different form. Only the naivete is gone, with the simplicity of ignorance replaced by a higher level of spirit and understanding. In short, the fire of the sun creates the stuff we are made of. Eventually the writer creates the deliciously flammable material he is made of; so too all the combustible material that makes up the idea of writing.

I applaud the format and structure of this book. This is a worthy addition to poetic and meditative literature and a joy to read. I am particularly moved by the skill of a poet who suggests the unknown, the mythical, the ethereal by using concrete images and human history in a straightforward way.

The poem, Lake Alma, offers an evocative landscape in which the people, like writing itself, are born to the land and die like the speechless wind. Like the sound and feel of the words that describe them, the memory of these 'spectre people' is reborn, many times as large, in the imagination of the reader.

Geoff Laundy, Author, poet, videographer

See and compare 'Ouroboros' note in Resources section

Compare **Heraclitus**:

> *"No man ever steps in*
> *the same river twice, for it's*
> *not the same river and*
> *he's not the same man."*

LL [4]

ACKNOWLEDGMENTS

It is with grace and humility that I express my gratitude to the people and the mystical and ethereal forces that have inspired and sustained me through this creative journey of life, learning, and spiritual awakening.

Thank you to the many people who I have met, worked with, loved, been loved by and have been the source of my inspiration, especially my parents. The influence of my now deceased wife, Judith Gill, appears in many of these poems.

A special thanks to my decades old, now reignited, 'affaire de Coeur'/ affaire d'amour, Daphne McDonald, who has provided so much perspective, encouragement, love, and inspiration. Many of my early poems and so many of the more recent have flowed from her inspiration. Without these, and her critical writer's eye, this book would not have been completed.

A very special thank you to my good friend of nearly four decades, and birthday brother, Jim Sellers, who offered his especially sharp eye and own appreciation of art and poetry in conception, proof-reading and critical insights to make this book the 'best that it can be'. Jim also provided meta-phorical perspective in his back-cover commentary.

I'm grateful also to my friends who offered perspectives, advice and encouragement: Geoff Laundy who wrote the inside cover commentary; Dr. Hon. Bernard Poulin, painter, sculptor, writer and teacher of international renown; my niece, Caroline Nevin, fine artist and creative writer, who both provided back-cover commentary, as well as long-time friend, Judy Bader.

Special thanks to Kent Swinburne whose very keen eye, insight and appreciation of poetry were important to making this a 'less imperfect' book. Thanks also to John Yarske, who wrote a compelling review of the personal impact the book had on him. Appreciation is also extended to Sylvia Nagy, who reacted similarly and provided valuable feedback. Thanks also to Lorraine Scory, David Grantham, and kindred spirits Elissa Michaud and Anthea Browne as well as other readers and reviewers.

Thanks to Jane Cannings, author and mentor to creative writers, who reviewed some poems and advised me to read my poems aloud to check cadence, suggesting that I might not hear what I thought I had written. Indeed!

So many experiences have influenced my life and provided the core foundation of my values and inspiration to leave the world a better place than when I entered. First, the example set by my parents within a Protestant community where familiarity bred trust, not betrayal.

An early read of Dag Hammarskjöld's Markings inspired me as did Kahlil Gibran's The Prophet, particularly the poem 'On Children' with its theme of guidance, not possession; Lawrence LeShan's The Medium, the Mystic and the Physicist; Abraham Maslow's hierarchy of needs; an early interest in Thermodynamics; and many others. Readers will see the influence of many poets/lyricists like Rod McKuen, Leonard Cohen and others cited in the themes explored in this book.

RESOURCES

Consistent with the basic premise of this book, that '**every beginning contains the seeds and signs of its own ending**', is the archetypal symbol of the **Ouroboros.** The Ouroborus is an ancient <u>symbol</u> depicting a <u>serpent</u> or <u>dragon</u> <u>eating its own tail</u>. Originating in <u>ancient Egyptian iconography</u>, the ouroboros entered western tradition via <u>Greek magical tradition</u> and was adopted as a symbol in <u>alchemy</u>.

Sir <u>Thomas Browne</u>. In his <u>A Letter to a Friend</u>, a medical treatise full of case-histories and witty speculations upon the human condition, he wrote of it: the first day should make the last, that the Tail of the Snake should return into its Mouth precisely at that time, and they should wind up upon the day of their Nativity.

Psychologist <u>Carl Jung</u> saw the ouroboros as an <u>archetype</u> and the basic <u>mandala</u> of alchemy. Jung also defined the relationship of the Ouroboros to alchemy. The alchemists, who in their own way knew more about the nature of the <u>individuation</u> process than we moderns do, expressed this paradox through the symbol of the Ouroboros, the snake that eats its own tail. The Ouroboros has been said to have a meaning of infinity or wholeness. In the age-old image of the Ouroboros lies the thought of devouring oneself and turning oneself into a circulatory process, for it was clear to the more astute alchemists that the prima materia of the art was man himself.* The Ouroboros is a dramatic symbol for the integration and assimilation of the opposite, i.e. of the shadow. This 'feed-back' process is at the same time a symbol of immortality, since it is said of the Ouroboros that he slays himself and brings himself to life, fertilizes himself and gives birth to himself. He symbolizes the One, who proceeds from the clash of opposites, and he therefore constitutes the secret of the prima materia which ... unquestionably stems from man's unconscious."

* See 'Afterword' by Geoff Laundy.
https://en.wikipedia.org/wiki/Ouroboros

'The Beautiful Benefits of Contemplating Doom', Virginia Heffernan, Ideas, Wired Magazine, 03.25.19. 4.7.19
https://www.wired.com/story/the-beautiful-benefits-of-contemplating-doom/

I encourage readers interested in the *'historical abuse and subjugation of women'*, discussed in Chapter 4, to do an internet search using that term. There are many sites that discuss this subject, from centuries old, male dominated cultures, the British Magna Carta 1215, and more recent recognition of women as persons under the law, voting rights, and the 'Me Too' movement. Many cultures are still in high states of denial of, and resistance to, recognizing the socio/economic/political realities of this and their devastating effects on women and society.

'Historical Roots of Sexual Oppression', Erwin J. Haeberle, http://huberlin. de/sexology/GESUND/ARCHIV/opress.htm

First published in: The Sexually Oppressed, Harvey L. Gochros and Jean S. Gochros (eds.), Association Press, New York, 1977, pp. 3-27 https://www. ipce.info/library/web-article/historical-roots-sexual-oppression

Construction of a Feminist Sexual Consciousness. Women's Sexual Consciousness and history of sexual oppression and https://www.youtube.com/watch?v=kmraIS_VDIA# Evin María Ximena Phoenix

A beautiful, poetic rebellion against such subjugation of women from Eileen Manassian Ghali's poem entitled "My Kind" was posted by her on poetrysoup.com.

Sexism: https://en.wikipedia.org/wiki/Sexism History, stereotypes, language, objectification and more.

The following books are among many that provide *contrasting views of love and sexuality*:

C.S. Lewis, The Four Loves, Hardcover – November 7, 1991 The Four Loves summarizes four kinds of human love--affection, friendship, **erotic love**, and **the love of God**. Masterful without being magisterial, this book's wise, gentle, candid reflections on the virtues and dangers of love draw on sources from **Jane Austen** to **St**. Augustine. Lewis's earlier book, Mere Christianity (citations EM 3) suggests similarities between the experience of 'being surprised by joy' and 'transcendence'.

The Myth of Monogamy: Fidelity and Infidelity in Animals and Humans, David Barash and Judith Lipton, First Holt Paperback sedition 2002, based on scientific research.

The Erotic Mind, Jack Morin, Ph.D. HarperCollins, Perennial Edition, 1996. "The Erotic Mind offers new and unexpected opportunities for intimate partners to appreciate the depth and richness of each other-and to translate their appreciation into passionate and fulfilling sex." Review by John Gray, author, Men are from Mars, Women are from Venus.

The State of Affairs: Rethinking Infidelity, Esther Perel, Psychotherapist, author, 2017, HarperCollins Publishers. "Love is a mess; infidelity more so," says Perel, which is an obvious and undeniable fact. Once trust has been lost due to an affair, is there truly a way to get it back? This is just one concern that the book tries to address by portraying the stories of real couples and their experience with infidelity."

Development of self-identity and consciousness

Lousy Sex, 2013 Gerald Callahan, 2013 University Press of Colorado, explores the science of self, illustrating the role of bacteria and the immune system in forming individual identity.

Mind and Cosmos: Why the Materialist Neo-Darwinian Conception of Nature is Almost Certainly False Thomas Nagel. 2012, Oxford University Press, contests the Darwinian mind-body duality and materialist view of human experience and explores the concept of transcendent experience reminiscent of Jung's 'collective unconscious' and Pierre de Chardin's 'noosphere'(as a fourth dimension along with time, space and matter).

The Mating Mind: How Sexual Choice Shaped the Evolution of Human Nature Geoffrey Miller. 2001 Anchor Books, Random House. Consciousness, morality, creativity, language, and art: these are the traits that make us human. Scientists have traditionally explained these qualities as merely a side effect of surplus brain size, but Miller argues that they were sexual attractors, not side effects. He bases his argument on Darwin's theory of sexual selection, which until now has played second fiddle to Darwin's theory of natural selection. It draws on ideas and research from a wide range of fields, including psychology, economics, history, and pop culture. Witty, powerfully argued, and continually thought-provoking, The Mating Mind is a landmark in our understanding of our own species.

Discounts are suitable for libraries, writer's and poetry groups, educators, corporations, gifts or for resale.

Readers interested in purchasing several copies of this book may contact me directly to obtain discounts for volume purchases of paperback books (no discounts on hard cover or e-books). The discounts are as follows:

5 to 10 copies: $1.00; 11 to 20 copies: $1.50 Additional discounts for larger volumes will be considered.
Please contact me at:
Email: mel.gill@synergyassociates.ca: https://www.facebook.com/mel.gill.90/about: www.synergyassociates.ca

CITATIONS

Some of the quotes cited in this book were gathered as many as sixty-five years ago. I started curating poems about age nine. Many were from 'Reader's Digest' and 'Lion's International Magazine'. Others were from books of poetry, history and English classes in middle and high school or university. Other quotes originated from authors' own websites and innumerable sites that contain quotes. Those that I have used most are: 'goodreads.com', 'all-poetry.com', 'brainyquote.com', 'quoteinvestigator.com', wordpress.com, 'pinterest.ca', and Wikipedia.

I have made all reasonable efforts to identify the original sources of quotations. Please contact me at mel.gill@synergyassociates.ca if you have any concerns about accuracy of sources or quotes.

The citations are organized within sections or chapters. Citations in the first section of the book from cover to the beginning of the first chapter are treated as one section with consecutive numbering. Each new chapter restarts its own sequence of numbers again starting with 1.

Cover to Intro (CI)

CI 1 Formation of Coral, Metamorphoses Book IV 8 A.D. Ovid (43 B.C. to 18 A.D.) Latin/Roman poet

CI 2 References to Greek Mythology, Mythology: Timeless Tales of Godz and Heroes, Edith Hamilton, Little Brown and Company, 1942. 75th Anniversary Edition, 2017 Black "Dog and Leventhal Publishers, Hatchet Book Group.

Making of a Poem (MP)

MP 3 Socrates (470-399 BC) one of the most influential Greek Philosophers, teacher of Plato, https://www.quotes.net/quote/950 Socrates left no written work. All the quotes and philosophical expressions were transcribed for him by Plato

MP 4 Nikola Tesla, Serbian-American engineer (1856–1943) futurist, inventor, Alternating electrical current (AC) https://www.goodreads.com/quotes/753175-my-brain-is-only-a-receiver-in-the-universe-there https://www.bing.com/images/search?q=imgurl%3ahttps%3a%2f%2fjeromeyers.files.wordpress.com%2f2012%2f10%2fnicolo-tesla-my-brain-is-only-a-receiver.jpg&view=detailv2&iss=sbi&rtpu=%2fsearch%3fq%3dnikola+tesla+%22My+brain+is+only+a+receiver.+&form=IEQNAI&selectedindex=0&id=https%3A%2F%2Fjeromeyers.files.wordpress.com%2F2012%2F10%2Fnicolo-tesla-my-brain-is-only-a-receiver.

jpg&mediaurl=https%3A%2F%2Fjeromeyers.files.wordpress.com%2F2012%2F10%2Fnicolo-tesla-my-brain-is-only-a-receiver.jpg&exph=0&expw=0&vt=0

MP 5 Mary Stevenson (1922-1999) Footprints, Official Website:
http://www.footprints-inthe-sand.com/index.php?page=Main.php Gail Giorgio,
Footprints in the Sand: The Inspiring Life Behind the Immortal Poem Paperback – 1997 Gold Leaf Pr
(May 1995)

MP 6 Dr. Hon. Laurentian University, Bernard Poulin (1945-), painter, poet, author, sculptor and teacher
of international renown, On Life, Death And Nude Painting, A Classic Perceptions Publication p.2.15

MP 7 Paul Simon, contemporary singer-songwriter, interview, Today Show, Oct 17, 2019 https://www.
bing.com/videos/search?q=Today+show+Oct+17+2018+Paul+Simon&view=detail&mid=6C29D87102C
0629331CD6C29D87102C0629331CD&FORM=VIRE

Introduction (IN)

IN 8 Lao Tzu (551-479 BC) Taoist Chinese philosopher, author of 'The Art of War', Tao Te Ching (The
Way: essential, unnamable process of the universe) influenced Confucianism and other Chinese philosophies

IN 9 The Holy Bible, RSV, Thomas Nelson & Sons, NY 1953, Revelation, 1.8

IN 10 Roger Whittaker, (1936-) Kenyan-born, British-based singer-songwriter and musician, 'The first
hello, the last goodbye' (1976) "The Last Farewell" Album 1988, numerous awards, 60 Million+ Albums sold

IN 11 E. E. Cummings (1894-1962) American poet, painter, essayist, author, and playwright, https://
leroywatson4.wordpress.com/2012/08/11/e-e-cummings-how-fortunate-are-you/

Chapter 1 Birth (CB)

CB 1 Lao Tzu, Tao Te Ching

CB 2 John Galsworthy (1867-1931) British author, playwright, poet, 1932 Nobel Prize in Literature,
Loyalties (Fifth Series) Kindle Edition, 2018 Createspace Independent Publishing Platform, NV USA

CB 3 Robert Service (1874-1958) The Collected Poems of Robert Service, 1907, G. P. Putnam's Sons NY

CB 4 Rudyard Kipling (1865-1936) Poet, author, Collected Poems of Rudyard Kipling (Wordsworth
Poetry Library) Paperback – 1999

CB 4 Kipling, Ibid.

CB 5 Saxon White Kessinger (1924-2005) American poet, 'The Indispensable Man' 1927, "The Nutmegger
Poetry Club under the name Saxon Uberuaga. It has also been published in "Boots" in Spring 1993, in "The
Country Courier" 1996, "Rhyme Time" in Winter 2000, and in "Golden Times" in August 2003.

Chapter 2 Parenting (CP)

CP 1 Kahlil Gibran (1883-1931) Lebanese American poet and visual artist, The Prophet, 1923 Alfred A.
Knof Inc. NY

CP 2 Lao Tzu, Tao Te Ching

CP 3 Gibran, Ibid.

CP 4 Kessinger, Ibid.

CP 5 Aristotle (384-322 B, C.) Greek Philosopher and Scientist, student of Plato, tutor to Alexander the Great, https://philosiblog.com/author/philosiblog 08.08.16; https://www.brainyquote.com/quotes/aristotle_400385

CP 6 Nelson Henderson (1865-1943) Scottish rugby player, author; https://grhgraph.wordpress.com/2009/08/21/the-true-meaning-of-life-is-to-plant-trees-under-whose-shade-you-do-not-expect-to-sit-nelson-henderson/

CP 7 Socrates, https://www.goodreads.com/quotes/69267-education-is-the-kindling-of-a-flame-not-the-filling of a vessel.

CP 8 Matthew L. Jacobson (1961-) Family Share, American author, Pastor, politician. https://www.thefreshquotes.com/parents-quotes/

CP 9 L.R. Knost (contemporary), Little Heart Books, author, feminist, social justice activist. https://www.goodreads.com/quotes/772398-for-a-child-it-is-in-the-simplicity-of-play

CP 10 L.R. Knost, Little Hearts Handbook series of gentle parenting guides. https://www.pinterest.ca/pin/200832464606137460/

Chapter 3 Love (CL)

CL 1 David Grayson, pen name for Ray Stannard Baker (1870-1946) Poet, Inspirational writer. Adventures in Contentment 2018 Trieste Publishing

CL 2 Eric Fromm (1900-1980) Social Psychologist, Psychotherapist, Philosopher, Art of Loving 1956 HarperCollins Publishers

CL 3 'Should You Share Your Sexual History with Your spouse?' https://www.marriagehelper.com/should_I_share_sexual_history_with_spouse.php

CL 4 Matthew Kelly (1973-) The Seven Levels of Intimacy Australian-born motivational speaker and business consultant

CL 5 Dorothy Tennov (1928-2007) American poet, Love and Limerence: The Experience of Being in Love 1999 Edition, (2nd Edition) Publisher: Scarborough House [Paperback] Paperback – Jan 13, 1999

CL 6 Plato, Greek Philosopher, 427-347 B.C. Pivotal figure in the development of Western philosophy https://www.goodreads.com/quotes/12860-

CL 7 William Shakespeare (1564-1616) English poet, play-write, actor, Bard of Avon, regarded as greatest writer in the English language, The Oxford Shakespeare: The Complete Sonnets and Poems, Edited by Colin Burrow.

CL 8 Bob Dylan (1941-) 'Times They are a Changin' lyrics; Nobel Laureate for Literature 2016 for a vast body of work. https://www.youtube.com/watch?v=kmraIS_VDIA#

CL 9 'Adultery: A Bizarre Legal History', http://www.duhaime.org/LegalResources/FamilyLaw/LawArticle-1626/Adultery-A-Bizarre-Legal-History.aspx.

CL 10 Matthew Kelly, Ibid.

CL 11 Plato, The Symposium, OXFORD University Press, Oxford NY, 1994. https://www.goodreads.com/book/show/81779.The_Symposium

CL 12 Lionel Richie (1949-), Singer, Song Writer - Endless Love, original movie soundtrack, 1981, Motown, Commodores, "We are the World" co-written with Michael Jackson, numerous music honors.

CL 13 'Leave me Breathless', July 2000, third studio album In Blue (2000), The Coors, Andrea Jane, Caroline, James & Sharon Corr & Robert John Lange

CL 14 'Somewhere My Love, Lara's Theme', 1965, Maurice Jarre (1924-2009) French music composer, giant of 20th century music/film industry, multiple 'Academy' and 'Globe' film awards [Lawrence of Arabia, Dr. Zhivago {Lara's Theme}, 1965 movie Dr. Zhivago]; excerpts from Lara's Theme.

Chapter 4 Sexuality and Erotica (SE)

SE 1 Julian Baggini, British writer, philosopher, 'Is there any real distinction between 'high' and 'low' pleasures?' How the World Thinks: A Global History of Philosophy (2018). GRANTA Publishing, Cambridge University, U.K.

SE 2 Rod McKuen (1933-2015), best-selling American poet, singer-songwriter, Grammy and Golden Globe Awards

SE 2 Leonard Cohen (1934-2016) Canadian singer-songwriter, poet and novelist, two Grammys, reputed to be one of the best contemporary lyricists in poetry and song: Leonard Cohen Selected Poems 1956-1968 Mass Market Paperback Viking; 1st Edition (June 26, 1968)

SE 2 Maurice Jarre, Ibid.

SE 3 Lee Hazlewood (1929-2007) American country and pop singer, songwriter, and record producer, 1968 Country Music award for vocal duo.

SE 4 Jenifer Rush 'Power of Love' (Jenifer Rush, (John Victor Colla, Huey Lewis, Christopher John Hayes) (1960-), opera-trained U.K. singer-songwriter, pop-rock singer, hugely successful in Europe.

SE 5 Obsessive Love, 1960, Eileen Manassian Ghali, Iranian-born, Armenian decent, Lebanese resident poet writes about women's entitlement to passion, equality, respect. Posted by her to poetrysoup.com.

SE 6 David Barash and Judith Lipton, The Myth of Monogamy: Fidelity and Infidelity in Animals and Humans, First Holt Paperback edition, W.H.Freeman, 2001, Henry Holt & Company New York, 2002, p.183.

SE 7 Barash and Lipton, Ibid. p. 201

SE 8 Ibid. pp. 191-192

SE 9 Zosia Bielski, 'Women are closing the infidelity gap:' New book explores why wives cheat, Globe Life, Relationships, October 1, 2018.

SE 10 Jeffrey Escoffier The Sexual Revolution, 1960-1980 by Encyclopedia Copyright © 2015, glbtq, Inc. https://en.wikipedia.org/wiki/Masters_and_Johnson#Criticisms; http://www.glbtqarchive.com/ssh/sexual_revolution_S.pdf;

SE 11 Robert Chartham, The Sensuous Couple 1971 Ballantine Books NY

SE 12 Alex Comfort, The Joy of Sex: A Gourmet Guide to Lovemaking 1972 Octopus Publishing Group originally published in the U.S. New York, Crown

SE 13 George and Nina O'Neill, Open Marriage: A New Lifestyle for Couples, M. Evans and Company Inc. 1972.

SE 14 Esther Perel, State of Affairs: Rethinking Infidelity HarperCollins Publishers, 2017 pp. 55, 92.

SE 15 Lizette Borelli, Paraphrase of article in Medical Daily, Hypersexual Disorder or Just a High Sex Drive? Profile of a Sex Addict. Mar 11, 2015 https://www.medicaldaily.com/hypersexual-disorder-or-just-high-sex-drive-profile-sex-addict-325198)
The premises of this article are affirmed by my own training and experience in mental health, child development, child welfare, and addictions.

SE 16 Dr. Robert Wiess, Psychotherapist, founder Sexual Healing Clinic, educator, author specializing in Infidelity, Betrayed Partners of Cheaters. Sex Addiction 101: A Basic Guide to Healing from Sex, Porn and Love Addiction, Public Health Communications Inc. and Dr. Fran Walfish, Psychotherapist, author: The Self-Aware Parent: Resolving Conflict and Building a Better Bond with Your Child, Palgrave MacMillan 2010, paraphrase of Lizette Borelli, Mar 11, 2015 article in Medical Daily

SE 17 Ethlie Ann Vare (1953-) Journalist, screenwriter, biographer, women's advocate, author: Love Addict: Sex, Romance and other Dangerous Drugs, Health Publications Inc. Deerfield Beach FL. Paperback, International Edition, 2011. Author of numerous other books and TV scripts (CSI, Andromeda and more)

SE 18 Shakespeare, Sonnet 129, The Complete Works of William Shakespeare (Knickerbocker Classics) Hardcover – October 10, 2014

SE 19 Esther Perel, Ibid. pp. 48,46

SE 20 John Naisbit Megatrends: Ten New Directions Transforming Our Lives Hardcover – October 27, 1982, Warner Books, Inc.; 1st edition (October 27, 1982)

Chapter 5 Colors and Emotions (CE)

CE 1 Eve's Bayou, 1997 movie, Trimark Pictures, screenplay by Kasi Lemmons

CE 2 Leonardo Da Vinci, 1452-1519, Renaissance Man, Polymath, mathematician, inventor, one of the greatest minds and painters of all time (Mona Lisa) Philosophical Maxims. Morals. Polemics and Speculations (circa 1476)

CE 3 Carlos Castaneda (1925-1998), Anthropologist, author of books on Yaqui 'Peyote Culture' and shamanism: Teachings of Don Juan, University of California Press, 1968

CE 4 Pablo Picasso (1881-1973) Spanish painter, sculptor, printmaker, ceramicist, stage designer, poet and playwright. Regarded as one of the most influential artists of the 20th century https://www.brainyquote.com/quotes/pablo_picasso_138525

CE 5 William P. Young (1955-) Born, Grande Prairie, AB, very commercially successful Canadian novelist and author, The Shack, 2007, Hatchett Book Group; Crossroads and Eve

CE 6 Author Unknown, attributed, without evidence, to Henry David Thoreau and Nathaniel Hawthorne (1817-1862), American essayist, transcendentalist, activist,

CE 7 Elie Wiesel (1928-2016) [on indifference]. US News & World Report, 27 October 1986, Jewish Holocaust activist, 1986 Nobel Peace Prize

CE 8 Vincent van Gogh, 1853-1890, Dutch Post-Impressionist painter extraordinaire, 860 paintings in the last two years of his short life, https://www.goodreads.com/quotes/17974-i-dream-my-painting-and-i-paint-my-dream

Chapter 6 Gifts of Nature (GN)

GN 1 Author unknown, Wild Woman Sisterhood, aimhappy.com, https://wearewildness.tumblr.com/post/140455527319/the-mountains-are-my-bones-the-rivers-my-veins

GM 2 Chief Seattle, 'Web of Life', The Island, 1972, Victoria B.C., attributed to Chief Seattle, but likely penned one hundred years later by Edward Perry. http://quanta-gaia.org/ChiefSeattle.html

Chapter 7 Hope and Inspiration (HI)

HI 1 Maria D. Robinson (?) Poet, author, From Birth to One, 2003, Open University Press. https://www.goodreads.com/book/show/4707728-from-birth-to-one

HI 2 Langston Hughes (1902-1967) American poet, social activist, jazz poet, Harlem Renaissance Man, The Collected Poems of Langston Hughes. New York: Knopf/Vintage, 1994 by the Estate of Langston Hughes

HI 3 Antoine de Saint-Exupéry (1900-1944) Honored French poet, aviator, author of The Little Prince

HI 4 Mulan 1998 film, Walt Disney Company

HI 5 Mary Stevenson, Ibid.

HI 6 Dr. Steve Maraboli (1975 -) Inspirational Speaker, Author, Behavioral Scientist, Life, the Truth, and Being Free 2009 Better Today Publishing; 2014 Createspace Independent Publishing Platform

HI 7 Frank McKinney Hubbard (1868-1930) American cartoonist, humorist, journalist, https://www.brainyquote.com/quotes/kin_hubbard_122773

HI 8 William Arthur (1819-1901) author of inspirational poems and meditations, https://www.goodreads.com/quotes/23950-the-pessimist-complains-about-the-wind-the-optimist-expects-it

HI 9 Will Rogers (1879-1935) 'Cowboy Philosopher', one of America's greatest political sages. Wise and Witty Sayings of a Great American Humorist Hardcover – Hallmark Editions; English Language edition 1969. Quotable Will Rogers, The Hardcover –Gibbs Smith, December 2005 Joseph Carter, Editor

HI 10 Eric Fromm, Ibid.

HI 11 Martin Luther King Jr. (1929-1968) American civil rights activist, and inspirational speaker; MLK Memorial, August 2011 https://www.thepeoplesview.net/main/epeoplesview.net/2011/08/out-of-mountain-of-dispair-stone-of.html

Chapter 8 Life's Little Lessons (LL)

LL 1 Socrates, as portrayed in 'Theaetetus' by Plato

LL 2 Will Rogers, The Adventures of Samuel L. Clemens Hardcover – Jerome Loving (author) March 31, 2010. University of California Press; First Edition March 31, 2010

LL 3 Mark Twain, Ibid.

LL 4 Heraclitus, (535-475 BCE) Pre-Socratic Greek philosopher https://en.wikipedia.org/wiki/Heraclitus

LL 5 'The American Ruling Class' – TV Documentary, 2007, John Kirby, Director and storyline, The Press and The Public Project

LL 6 Aldous Huxley (1894-1963) English writer and philosopher, Brave New World, The Doors of Perception, Island, Point, Point Counter, and more. He also inspired George Orwell (1903-1950) English social democrat, novelist, poet and essayist, 1984 and Animal Farm.

LL 7 Gautama Siddhartha (Sanskrit), (483/400 BCE) the Buddha, mendicant, philosopher, sage, teacher, religious leader

LL 8 John Muir (1838-1914) Scottish-American naturalist, author, early advocate for the preservation of wilderness
https://www.adventure-journal.com/2013/10/the-aj-list-20-inspiring-quotes-from-john-muir/Oct 22, 2013

LL 9 Lao Tzu, Ibid.

LL 10 Mark Twain, Ibid.

LL 11 Robert Anthony American (1916-2006) business professor, Beyond Positive Thinking: A No-Nonsense Formula for Getting the Results You Want Paperback – Aug 2004 and other books. https://www.brainyquote.com/quotes/robert_anthony_125911

LL 12 Will Rogers, Jerome Loving, Ibid.

LL 13 Jack London (1876-1916) American Journalist, novelist, science fiction writer and social activist; Call of the Wild, White Fang, Star Rover and many others

LL 14 Josh Billings, (1818-1885) humorist, Mark Twain contemporary. This quote has been variously ascribed to Billings, Twain and others. There is no concrete evidence of the original source so, it is perhaps more correctly ascribed to 'author unknown. https://quoteinvestigator.com/2018/11/18/know-trouble/

LL 15 Ashley Montague (1905-1999) British American anthropologist noted for his works popularizing anthropology and science and integrating sciences, book and 1980 movie, "Elephant Man"; activist against discrimination (handicapped, women, race), authored more than 60 books. https://www.brainyquote.com/quotes/ashley_montagu_102365

LL 16 Richard Feynman (1918-1988) 1965 Nobel Laureate in Physics for work on quantum thermodynamics, particle physics, and development of atomic bomb. Richard P. Feynman Quotes. (n.d.). BrainyQuote.com. Retrieved April 19, 2019, from BrainyQuote.com Web site: https://www.brainyquote.com/quotes/richard_p_feynman_137642

LL 17 D. G. Altman, J. M. Bland, Argument from Ignorance, fallacy in logic.
BMJ. 1995 Aug 19; 311(7003): 485. PMCID: PMC2550545

LL 18 Author Unknown

LL 19 Paulo Friere (1921-1997) Brazilian Priest, Pedagogy of the Oppressed, Myra Bergman Ramos (Translator) Donaldo Macedo, Paperback, 30th Anniversary Edition, 192 pages, Published September 1, 2000 by Bloomsbury Academic (first published 1968)

LL 20 Attributed to Abraham Maslow's 'law of the instrument' or 'Golden Hammer' The Psychology of Science: A Reconnaissance 1966 New York Harper & Row. https://quoteinvestigator.com/2014/05/08/hammer-nail/

LL 21 Sir Francis Bacon (1561–1626) British Lord Chancellor, English Lawyer and Philosopher, , developed scientific method. http://thinkexist.com/quotes/with/keyword/narrowed/

Chapter 9 Existential Moments (EM)

EM 1 Sri Nisargadatta Maharaj, Hindu guru of nondualism (1897-1981) I Am That Part 12 (1999-08-19) Hardcover – 1644

EM 2 Henry David Thoreau Walden; or, Life in the Woods Paperback – Unabridged, Apr 12, 1995, Wisehouse Classics, Sweden

EM 3 C.S. Lewis (1898-1963) Mere Christianity Paperback edition 1996 Touchstone Press. Author, lay theologian, Professor of English Literature Oxford and Cambridge, Chronicles of Narnia, Screwtape Letters and many others.

EM 4 Ashley Montague, Ibid.

EM 5 Kahlil Gibran, Ibid.

EM 6 The Holy Bible, Mathew 6:22, Ibid.

EM 7 Mel Gill, Leonard Cohen. Inspired by Rumi, 13th-century Persian poet and mystic; later popularized by Leonard Cohen (1934-2016) substituting 'crack' for 'wound' Leonard Cohen, Selected Poems, 1956-1968 Mass Market Paperback – June 1, 1968, 'Anthem' "The Future" album, 1992

EM 8 Mary Oliver (1935-2019) The Uses of Sorrow Thirst, 2007. Beacon Press. American poet, Pulitzer Prize for Poetry (1984)

EM 9 Anonymous, misattributed to Bertrand Russell and G.B. Shaw. No evidence either said or wrote this. Many other possibilities including Carnegie and Churchill. https://quoteinvestigator.com/2015/10/10/war-not/

EM 10 George Santayana "Soliloquies in England" Charles Scribner's Sons New York 1924, p. 102), Soliloquy #25, "Tipperary" Paperback – Jun 5 2011 Attributed to Plato without evidence https://www.plato-dialogues.org/faq/faq008.htm.

Chapter 10 Growing Old (GO)

GO 1 Gabriel García Márquez (Gabo) (1917-2014) Nobel Prize in Literature, 1982 Memories of My Melancholy Whores 2014 Vintage International

GO 2 Bonnie Hunt (1961-) American comedienne, actress, voice artist, director, producer, writer and television host. https://www.goodreads.com/quotes/248308-just-cause-there-s-snow-on-the-roof-doesn-t-mean-there-s

GO 3 Mark Twain, Ibid.

GO 4 Will Rogers, Ibid.

GO 5 Matt Haig, (1975-) British novelist and journalist Reasons to Stay Alive How to Stop Time Paperback – Jan 19, 2016 Harper Avenue

Chapter 11 Dying and Death (DD)

DD 1 Carlos Castenada, The teachings of Don Juan: A Yaqui Way Of Knowledge Mass Market Paperback – Mar 3 1985 Washington Square Press Publication, Pocket Books, Simon & Schuster Inc. N.Y.

DD 2 Eric Fromm, Ibid.

DD 3 Ashley Montague, Ibid.

DD 4 Lord Byron (1788-1824) Poet, Peer, Politician, Romanticist https://www.brainyquote.com/quotes/lord_byron_377089

DD 5 Mark Twain, Ibid.

DD 6 Will Rogers, Ibid.

DD 7 Lao Tzu, Ibid.

DD 8 [8] James Russell Lowell (1818-1891) Romantic poet, diplomat, abolitionist. 'Of the Dawn of Freedom' poem https://www.poemhunter.com/poem/of-the-dawn-of-freedom/

DD 9 Stephen Hawking (1942-2018) Theoretical Physicist, Cosmologist. His theory of exploding black holes drew upon both relativity theory and quantum mechanics, author-Brief History of Time, Mind over Matter and others.

DD 10 Vladimir Nabokov (1899-1977) Speak, Memory (1951) pp.1-3. Russian-born novelist, poet, recognized as one of the finest novelists of his time. His many novels include Pale Fire and Lolita for which he won the 1963 Academy Award for Best Adapted Screenplay

DD 11 Dr. Steve Maraboli, Ibid.

DD 12 Jack London, Ibid.

DD 13 Aldous Huxley, Ibid.

DD 14 Plato, Ibid.

DD 15 'The Indispensable Man' Saxon White Kissinger, (1924-2005) American poet

DD 16 Gabriel García Márquez Love in the Time of Cholera Hardcover – Sep 16 1997 Nicholas Shakespeare (Introduction), Edith Grossman (Translator) Alfred A. Knopf, a division of Random House, N.Y.

End Note 17 Gayle McDonald Globe and Mail, Mar 15/18

ABOUT THE AUTHOR

Mel Gill, author, poet, researcher and consultant in governance and organizational development, divides his time between Ottawa, ON and Victoria, BC. He was married to his now deceased wife, Judith, of fifty years. They had two sons and two grandchildren. He currently lives with his youngest son, Trent, and their 'Chocolate Labrador Retriever'. Mel credits the experience of living with his adult son and a pet for providing deeper self-understanding and insight into the behavior of humans and other animals.

Mel's passions include readings on human behavior, philosophy, religion, quantum thermodynamics and other topics. He and his son are avid tournament bass anglers.

He and his first love from more than fifty years ago, Daphne McDonald, have reignited their passion for each other, life, living, and shared interests experienced in parallel paths. Their song, 'Somewhere My Love', from Lara's theme in the movie, Dr. Zivago, is a musical simulation of their re-encounter.

CPSIA information can be obtained
at www.ICGtesting.com
Printed in the USA
LVHW031907170919
631412LV00001B/1